# MARCO ⊕ POLO

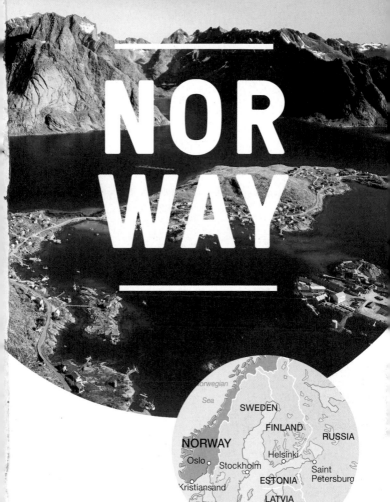

# NOR WAY

SWEDEN

FINLAND

RUSSIA

NORWAY

Oslo  Stockholm   Helsinki

Saint
Petersburg

Kristiansand   ESTONIA

DEN-
MARK   LATVIA

LITHUANIA

RUS  BELARUS

Norwegian
Sea

T0150569

www.marco-polo.co

FREE!

# THE
# TOURING APP

shows you the way ...
including routes and offline maps!

# GET MORE OUT OF YOUR MARCO POLO GUIDE

IT'S AS SIMPLE AS THIS

**1** go.marco-polo.com/nor

**2** download and discover

# GO!

WORKS OFFLINE!

**SYMBOLS**

INSIDER TIP ▶ Insider Tip

★ Highlight

●●●● Best of...

☼ Scenic view

♲ Responsible travel: for ecological or fair trade aspects

(*) Telephone numbers
that are not toll-free

**PRICE CATEGORIES
HOTELS**

*Expensive* over 1,450 NOK

*Moderate* 1,050–1,450 NOK

*Budget* under 1,050 NOK

Prices for two in a double
room per night, with breakfast

**PRICE CATEGORIES
RESTAURANTS**

*Expensive* over 480 NOK

*Moderate* 335–480 NOK

*Budget* under 335 NOK

Prices are for a meal with a
starter, main course and des-
sert, as well as a soft drink,
but without any alcohol

On the cover: Geiranger fjord p. 51 | Glacial lakes at Jostedalsbreen p. 115

# CONTENTS

---

**DID YOU KNOW?**
Timeline → p. 14
No. 1 in one-night stands → p. 24
Local specialities → p. 28
Dark days, bright nights → p. 74
For bookworms & film buffs → p. 77
National holidays → p. 121
Budgeting → p. 126
Currency converter → p. 128
Weather → p. 129

**MAPS IN THE GUIDEBOOK**
(136 A1) Page numbers and coordinates refer to the road atlas
(O) Site/address located off the map.
Coordinates are also given for places that are not marked on the road atlas
(U A1) Refers to the city map of Oslo inside the back cover

(*A–B 2–3*) refers to the removable pull-out map
(*a–b 2–3*) refers to the in-set map on the pull-out map

**INSIDE FRONT COVER:**
The best Highlights

**INSIDE BACK COVER:**
Oslo city map

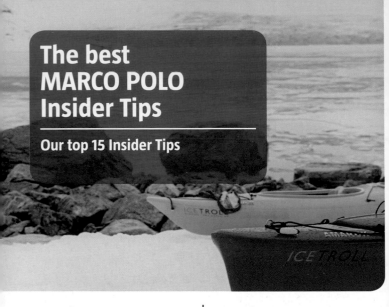

# The best MARCO POLO Insider Tips

## Our top 15 Insider Tips

**INSIDER TIP Artistic knitwear**

For a present or to treat yourself: the knitted sweaters and cardigans by *Oleana* will bring the special Nordic tradition and culture back to your home. The swirling rose patterns are inspired by the decorations on old fishing boats → **p. 31**

**INSIDER TIP Fish with finesse**

In Bergen, fresh regional ingredients include the best that the sea has to offer. Try the tasty delights whipped up by the award-winning chef Hanne Froste at the restaurant *Marg & Bein* as she does wonders with fish and seaweed → **p. 55**

**INSIDER TIP Polynesian bar for night owls**

Named after Thor Heyerdahl's book on his explorations of Easter Island, the *Aku-Aku Tiki Bar* in Oslo's district Grünerløkka has Polynesian memorabilia, dancing hula girls and great-tasting cocktails → **p. 45**

**INSIDER TIP A change of climate**

The Jotunheimen *Klimapark 2469* is located high up in the mountains. Discover an unknown world in a glacier tunnel that definitely proves one thing: it's getting warmer → **p. 35**

**INSIDER TIP With the miners on Spitsbergen**

The former miners' canteen might now be a dining room, but just beyond *Coal Miners' Cabin* on Svalbard, the realm of the polar bears still beckons → **p. 87**

**INSIDER TIP Delicious bread in the fjell**

A first-class Norwegian chef bakes the best bread north of the Skagerrak in *Bakeriet i Lom* → **p. 36**

**INSIDER TIP Perfect Norwegian fjords**

The ship steams from the majestic Sognefjord towards the snow-covered mountains and glaciers – and everybody on the *ferry from Balestrand to Fjærland* (photo right) remains on deck → **p. 60**

**INSIDER TIP** **Artisanal beer**

The small village of Flåm is not only home to the world-famous railway line but also the country's most authentic craft brewery. Enjoy one of their beers in the pub belonging to the *Ægir microbrewery* → **p. 111**

**INSIDER TIP** **All in a spin**

Feel free to wash your dirty laundry in public at the *Café Laundromat* in Oslo. Enjoy a milky coffee and pancake while you wait → **p. 44**

**INSIDER TIP** **Paddling between sea ice**

Wrapped up warmly, you can paddle across the *glacial lakes at Jostedalsbreen* in a kayak – an exhilarating experience (photo left) → **p. 115**

**INSIDER TIP** **A protected power plant to explore**

The magnificent *Norwegian Museum of Hydropower and Industry* in Tyssedal tells the story of technical progress → **p. 105**

**INSIDER TIP** **Sleep and read**

Live like a Norwegian grandfather who fished on the Arctic Sea in the two houses belonging to *Bed & Books* in Tromsø. Plus, your fellow guests will most likely come from all over the world → **p. 90**

**INSIDER TIP** **Marked by the Arctic Ocean**

The deserted village of *Hammingberg* lies at the end of the world. The 35 km/22 miles route to get there takes you along the eastern Barents Sea – a trip you will never forget → **p. 98**

**INSIDER TIP** **An island for all the senses**

The island of *Træna* lies a long way off the coast of Norway. Nothing disturbs the peace here – except on three days in July when the music at the rock festival drowns out the sound of the sea and gulls → **p. 77**

**INSIDER TIP** **Ancient recipes**

If you want to take some of the best smoked salmon home with you, you should drop by the *Jans Fiskerøykeri* in Stavanger → **p. 62**

# BEST OF...

**FOR FREE**

● *Bird's eye view*
The most spectacular view in mainland Norway costs nothing. Just walk out to the edge of the *Stegastein Lookout*, a viewing platform that resembles a ski jump at a dizzying height of 650 m (2,133 ft). If you're not afraid of heights, you'll definitely enjoy this unforgettable view of the Aurlandsfjord → p. 61

● *Twisting your way up the coast*
Toll booths may be familiar sights – but not on the *Atlantic Ocean Route*, perhaps the most unusual road to explore in Norway. The road snakes its way along the coast over bridges and islands: you can even fish from lay-bys and the gusts of wind make you think you're at sea → p. 60

● *Monumental art in the park*
Art appreciation with a picnic atmosphere: take your time to admire the famous sculptures in the *Vigelandsparken* (photo), which belongs to Frøgnerpark, one of the most popular places in the capital for meeting up with friends in the summer → p. 44

● *Fortress with a view*
You should not miss out on a view of the Oslofjord from the *Åkershus Fortress*. You have to pay to get into the palace with the royal mausoleum but you can visit the fortress complex for free → p. 41

● *City hall full of paintings*
The interior of Oslo's *Rådhuset* is decorated with friezes, murals and paintaings done by Norway's most famous artists. You probably won't get closer to the Nobel Peace Price than in this building: The award ceremony is held here on December 10 every year → p. 44

● *Memorial up in the north*
Although it cost 10 million euros to build, the *Steilneset Minnested memorial* in Vardø is free to visit. Designed by the Swiss artist Peter Zumthor, the monument stands as a reminder of Norway's witch hunting past → p. 98

( X X X ● ) Dots in guidebook refer to "Best of..." tips

# ONLY IN NORWAY
## Unique experiences

● *National pride*
Fresh birch twigs are an essential part of the Norwegian national holiday on 17 May, *Constitution Day*. If you can, try to be in Oslo on that day (photo). The celebrations in the capital are especially charming with a children's procession concluding the festivities → p. 120

● *The more extreme the better*
Thousands battle their way through the forests and over the mountains from Rena to Lillehammer on skis, bikes or even on foot as part of the *Birkebeiner Long Distance Race*. Join in if you feel fit enough: extreme sports are the done thing in Norway! → p. 114

● *Perfect craftsmanship*
The early days of Christianity in Norway have left magnificent reminders of that time: the stave churches with their – partially heathen – decoration. On no account should you miss the famous *Borgund Stavkirke* near Lærdal on the Sognefjord → p. 60

● *The winter sports' experience*
Not interested in ski jumping? You don't have to be to enjoy a visit the *Holmenkollen Ski Jump*. It holds the same place in the hearts of ski-jumpers as the Scala in Milan does with opera buffs. Visit the Ski Museum – and you will be breathless when you see the magnificent view → p. 42

● *Carved out in the Ice Age*
Norway's fjords are the missing link between the coast and the fjell. If you visit one of the most beautiful arms of the sea – the Lysefjord near Stavanger with its breathtaking rock plateau *Preikestolen* (photo) – you will see what is above and below, the sky and the water, in a completely new light – literally → p. 63

● *Epic on the sea*
When Norwegians talk about Norwegians, they almost always mention Peer Gynt. This hero in Henrik Ibsen's dramatic play is the embodiment of the way Norwegians see themselves: adventurous but narrow-minded, imaginative but absolutely realistic. For a classic performance, head to the *Peer Gynt- estival* held in the unbelievably beautiful countryside around Gålåvatnet Lake → p. 41

ONLY IN

# BEST OF...

## AND IF IT RAINS?
Activities to brighten your day

### ● Bad weather hideout
The *Hjerterommet* café in the centre of Bodø is like a home from home and a cosy retreat for body and soul → **p. 73**

### ● Penguins and crocodiles
Creatures that live in or near the water have found a new home in the *Akvariet* in Bergen. You will not only come across penguins and seals in the aquarium, but also snakes and crocodiles → **p. 52**

### ● Under glass
The ruins of the cathedral are the main attraction in the *Hedmarksmuseet* in Hamar. The impressive glass pyramid will also protect you from the elements – and let you experience the special atmosphere of the place undisturbed (photo) → **p. 40**

### ● The treasure in the silver mountain
Travel an exciting 2.3 km (1.4 mile) into the heart of the mountain with the pit railway of the *Norwegian Mining Museum* that runs through Kongsberg's old silver mine → **p. 46**

### ● Hunt, shop, look
You can outwit the bad weather in the *Devoldfabrikken* in Ålesund. Here, you will not only find the famous Devold pullovers but also lots of other items if you take the time to look around. And then there is the café with a wonderful view of the islands offshore... → **p. 50**

### ● The fascination of the fjell
Mountains near the Arctic Circle are a harsh environment for people, animals and plants to survive – and it was a long way from hunters and gatherers to modern tourists with their high-tech equipment. All of this is shown in the *Norsk Fjellmuseum* in Lom → **p. 36**

# RELAX AND CHILL OUT
## Take it easy and spoil yourself

● *Regal relaxation*
The *Holmenkollen Park Hotel* in Oslo is a fairy-tale palatial hotel with a health spa oasis and unbelievably beautiful view over the capital city and its fjord. Each minute in the hotel, each titbit in the restaurant – pure indulgence and pleasure → **p. 45**

● *A cruise in an open-air cinema*
You will spend as much time as possible on deck relaxing, reading, taking photos or just watching the scenery. As the ship glides past fjords, peaks and islands, more islets, reefs and skerries appear on the horizon. A trip on one of the *Hurtigruten* ships is like being in a gigantic open-air cinema featuring a feast for all the senses → **p. 24**

● *The light of Jæren*
Beautiful beaches, dunes and the murmur of the waves: an almost un-Norwegian environment awaits you in the *Sola Strand Hotel* south of Stavanger. Swimming pool, sauna and related spa facilities top off this relaxing experience → **p. 63**

● *Steam bath in the North Sea*
If you've made it up to Bodø, you should treat yourself to a few hours in the *Nordlandsbadet* with its whirlpools, herbal steam bath and sauna – a pleasure for body, mind and soul → **p. 74**

● *A steamer to the slopes*
The Telemark is really a synonym for winter sports. But, you can also discover the sporting region in comfort on board one of the two old steamers *Victoria* and *Henrik Ibsen* → **p. 46**

● *Forest retreat*
Forget wellness temples: plunge into the hot whirlpool at *The Well* and enjoy the fantastic views over the pine forest. The ultimate in peace, tranquility and relaxation just to the south of Oslo → **p. 115**

INTRODUCTION

# DISCOVER
# NORWAY!

The world eagerly turns its attention to this country situated in the northern corner of Europe at least once a year when the recipient of the *Nobel Peace Prize* is announced. Norway, a discrete, unassuming country but with a lot to offer. An observation shared by the inventor of dynamite, Alfred Nobel, who bequeathed his fortune to institute the Nobel Prizes. He specified on his death that all the prizes should be awarded in Stockholm except for the prize for world peace (a way for Alfred Nobel to settle his bad conscience), which should be administered in Oslo (ruled in union with Sweden at the time of Nobel's death). Since then, the Norwegians have acted as a world chief over the global community. Each year the prize aims to shed light on a particular crisis and – in the case of the Chinese dissident Liu Xiaobo – is not a stranger to controversy.

The country does not have to go looking for friends; they come on their own. Norway is ranked number one in many lists: the country with the least corruption, the *best quality of life*, and the most advanced climate policies – these best-in-the-class Norwegians are showing the rest of the world how it's done. But that's not all. They even have a likeable Royal Family and women who go out to work while their hub-

The place to be seen on a summer evening – Aker Brygge on the Oslofjord

bies stay at home to look after the baby. This level of affluence and well-being can be off putting at first, especially to onlookers. Admit it: it's easy to be a tiny bit jealous of this near-perfect nation. But resist the temptation. Justify it by saying they deserve it. If oil had never been discovered off the Norwegian coastline at the end of the 1960s, the *oljeeventyr* – or their *"oil fairytale"* – would never have begun. Norway would have remained Europe's poor Nordic neighbours with nothing to show but its unspoilt natural beauty.

The oil boom enabled the country to harvest the enormous sums of money in its deeply rooted *social democracy and egalitarian policies*, a Nordic value reflected in *Janteloven* – or the *Law of Jante* – a sociological term to describe a belief that nobody is better than anyone else. The money generated from oil and gas (Nor-

**8000 BC**
At the end of the Ice Age, the first people follow reindeer and other game to the north

**1500–500 BC**
Bronze Age. Farming dominates in the south and hunting in the north

**793–1066**
Viking era. Harald "Beautiful Hair" unites large sections of Norway in 872

**c. 1250**
The Hanseatic League establishes outposts and exploits the country

**1349–50**
The plague kills 50 to 60 percent of the population

way is still the world's fifth largest exporter of oil and Europe's second largest exporter of gas) is invested into a *giant sovereign wealth fund*, and the country has virtually no debt whatsoever. One of the major challenges through the century has been to connect up this vast, and in many regions, desolate country. Its broadband connectivity is a resounding success; there is even a mobile connection in the most isolated fjell. However its transportation infrastructure has proved more arduous due to its convoluted coastline of fjords and mountains: roads and railways are still under construction between Fredrikstad and Kirkenes, bridges are being built over the fjord to partly replace the ferries while tunnels are continually drilled into the country's seemingly endless mountain ranges. When it comes to *building tunnels*, the Norwegians lead the way: the country boasts 1100 tunnels, 30 of which are under water. Norway also holds the record for the world's longest road tunnel – the Lærdaltunnel which is 24.5 km/15 miles long.

Enough about traffic and transportation though; that's not the real reason for visiting Norway. Tourists come for the landscape – some regions where by the look of them no human has ever set foot. A *paradise for nature lovers* with spare mountains and desolate plateaus, home to herds of musk ox, reindeer and elk. Sea eagles can be spotted encircling the convoluted coastline and sperm whales are attracted by the warm Gulf Stream in the North Sea. In winter the soul-stirring *Northern Lights* are an exhilarating experience. You can spend literally weeks hiking through the landscape without meeting a soul – an experience sought by some natives looking to escape the hectic of modern life. Even Norway cannot halt the process of *urbanisation*: While four out of five

> **Norway is showing the rest of the world how it's done**

Norwegians live in cities or larger towns, the municipality of Kautokeino in the Finnmark county is home to just 3000 inhabitants scattered over an area almost six times the size of London. The further you get away from the larger towns and cities, the friendlier and more open the people seem to become. They lose some of their Nordic reserve as well as their inhibitions. Far away from the King's residence in the south, the language also becomes less restrictive – the *Northern Norwegian dialect* is known for its string of expletives.

**1397–1523**
Kalmar Union between Denmark, Sweden and Norway

**1814**
Denmark cedes Norway to Sweden (union until 1905). The Norwegian constitution is adopted on 17 May in Eidsvoll

**1940–45**
Occupation of Norway by the German Wehrmacht

**Mid-1960s**
First promising oil discoveries in the North Sea

**1972**
EU referendum: 53 percent of the Norwegians vote against membership

If you want to explore the *wildlife and wilderness*, it's good to know that nature will not let you starve in Norway: the fjords and rivers offer an abundance of fish, the mountains have a rich supply of clear fresh water and, depending on the season, the countryside is full of mushrooms and berries. From an early age, Norwegian children are taught to respect the nature around them. They regularly spend their weekends hiking and skiing and they quickly learn that *nature can be unpredictable*. The warm sun can suddenly turn into strong winds and rain showers. While the Gulf Stream keeps the coastal region humid throughout winter, temperatures inland can drop to minus 40 degrees. There is no such thing as bad weather, just poor clothing. In short, Norwegians don't let the weather spoil their fun. A popular national outdoor pastime at any time of year is barbecuing – an unforgettable experience under the *midnight sun*.

> ## Unforgettable experience: barbecuing under the midnight sun

Norwegians are often envied for their relaxed and laid-back temperament. How else can you expect them to behave in a country where it takes over eight hours to travel a distance of 500km/310 miles by car? Time is relative and instead of getting hot under the collar, Norwegians respond with a shrug of the shoulders and the matter is already forgotten. This behaviour stems from their basic need of *living together in harmony*. It gives them security and the feeling of living in an open and free society. King Harald appealed to his nation to show this same openness to foreigners in his speech in 2016: "Norway is above all its people. It is not always easy to say where we come from, to which nationality we belong. Home is where the heart is. That cannot always be placed within country borders."

Their *National Holiday on 17 May* is when adults act like children for the day and children learn to express their national pride. Many dress up in their national costume, the *bunad,* and sing their national anthem at the top of their voices at parades and processions: *Ja, vi elsker dette landet* – yes, we love this country. The Royal Family waves from their palace balcony and then there is ice cream for everyone followed by a family party in their own back garden. They are not only

**1991**
Harald V crowned king

**1994**
Second Norwegian "no" to EU membership

**22 July 2011**
77 people are killed in a terrorist attack in Oslo and on Utøya. The perpetrator was entenced to a lifetime term in prison in 2012

**2016**
Norway announces its intention of becoming climate neutral by 2030

**2017**
The Norwegian *pensjonsfond,* the world's largest sovereign wealth fund, exceeds the 1 billion dollar mark (approx. 834 billion euros)

celebrating their *independence* from Sweden but also the European Union, having voted twice against joining with a polite "thanks, but no thanks", or *nei, takk* in Norwegian.

A herd of reindeer galloping through the powder snow

This national pride was dinted only once in history in 2011 when the far-right extremist Anders Behring Breivik committed an *attack* on the island of Utøya off the coast of Oslo killing 77 mainly young people. This shooting left the

> **A small country and a proud people, who will never give up its values**

country shocked to its core and it united together in deep mourning. The Minister President at the time, Jens Stoltenberg, later the Secretary General of NATO, was deeply affected, saying: "We are a small country, but a *proud people*. We are still shocked by what has happened, but we will never give up our values. Our response is more democracy, more openness, and more humanity. But never naivety."

You can never accuse the Norwegians of being naive, yet quietly proud of having the good fortune to be blessed with affluence, a landscape of stunning beauty and political freedom. Immerse yourself into this land of plenty and appreciate its *way of life*!

# WHAT'S HOT

## 1 Street art

***Spray cans and stencils*** The best street artists in Norway have travelled all the way up to the Arctic Ocean, changing the face of abandoned villages, houses and industrial businesses as they go. Some of their critical commentaries on the present state of affairs have attracted international attention and the Italian documentary filmmaker Davide Fasolo has even done a film about the project of the artists Pöbel and Dolk on Lofoten. Check out *www.facebook.com/Komafest* and *fro emartinsen.blogspot.de/2011/06/ dolk-og-pbel-i-lofoten.html.*

## Icy experience

## 2

***Afraid of heights?*** Team-building is popular at the moment, and in Norway, the preferred venues are rapids or icy waterfalls. Rjukan is one of the trendiest places for ice-climbers. You book tours with incredibly experienced climbers from *Rjukan Adventure (www. rjukanadventure.no)*. The Hydnefossen Waterfall in Hemsedal and the waterfalls near Lærdal also offer superb climbing conditions. *Norske Opplevelser (www.nor skeopplevelser.no) (photo)* can provide you with know-how and group climbs. *Upptur (www.upp.no)* offers excursions and ice-canyoning suitable for beginners and children.

## 3 Conscience in a bottle

***Juice from Oslo's gardens*** Norwegians love their home-made regional food and produce and are always keen to support social causes. So when a projectcomes along which cleverly combines both, it is a sure-fire winner. The latest product to hit the shelves is *Epleslang (www.epleslang.com)*. The apple juice is made from surplus apples from Oslo's gardens and harvested by people with mental and physical disabilities.

# Music country

*Out into the country* Norway's music fans have claimed the countryside for themselves. Weekends in summer are filled with rock or pop festivals held between boat houses and as close to the water as possible. Big celebrities or international stars are not important. Rather, the relatively young audiences, who otherwise delight in the joys of the city, love the change of scenery and the simplicity of life in a tent or basic accommodation when they attend these festivals dotted across the countryside. Towns like Øystese *(byg dalarm.no)* and Nordfjordeid *(mala-koff.no)* in western Norway as well as Tromøya island near Arendal *(hovefesti valen.no)* and the village of Kåfjord *(riddu. no)* in northern Norway are being kept afloat by the fresh musical wind coming from the big cities that blows over them once a year.

# Second hand

*High-end jumble sales* One man's rubbish is another man's treasure: second hand is in trend and there are bargains to be had in a country whose inhabitants share a passion for brand name clothing. Schools organise jumble sales twice a year where you can find everything from ski equipment to suitcases. Simply follow the signs showing *loppemarked*. The Internet is the biggest trader of second-hand goods: *www.finn.no* (only in Norwegian) is Norway's largest platform selling everything from outboard motors to designer handbags. Pets looking for a new home are also advertised on this website. If you prefer to look and touch before buying, head to *Fretex (www.fretex. no)*, the Salvation Army stores, which offer items of clothing and interior goods for sale.

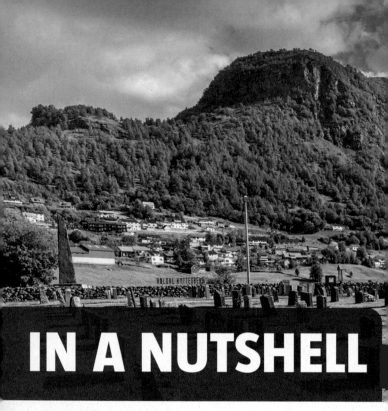

# IN A NUTSHELL

## JUMBO PIGGY BANK

If the national *pensjonsfond* – or state pension fund – was paid out today, it would equate to over 169,000 euros for each of Norway's 5.2 million citizens. A nice thought which Norwegians like to ponder on now and again. However instead of cashing them in, the funds, established in 1990 to invest all surplus revenues from the oil and gas industry, are saved to secure the prosperity of generations to come. One thing is clear: these vast oil reserves will unfortunately run dry at some point and the country's economic mainstay will have to be replaced by other alternatives. With or without oil though – the country's wealth lies at sea. Norway is the second largest supplier of salmon, trout and other fish.

However rather than drawing on nature's resources, the country has invested in commercial aquaculture to satisfy the enormous demand for Norwegian fish, whether it be in the Portuguese national dish Bacalao in Rio, in sophisticated cuisine in Paris or for sushi in Tokyo.

## STAVE CHURCHES: ALL WOOD AND BEAUTY

The oldest examples of the remaining 28 stave churches are approximately 1000 years old yet are as fascinating as ever, especially the Viking carvings which adorn the chapels: rooftop figures of dragons, snakes winding up the door posts – pagan symbols to protect Christianity. Their charm lies in the intelligent architectural structure: Made en-

Photo: Røldal stave church

We have sieved out the clichés, separating the facts from fiction. Find your special "a-ha moment" amongst them

tirely out of wood without any nails or screws, the construction is held up by neatly joined wooden posts and a stone foundation to protect the wooden structure from rotting underneath. The plain and unadorned interior is characterised by remnants of soot, testimony to the countless mass services and congregations held inside them. Examples of magnificent and well-preserved stave churches can be seen in Borgund (Lærdal), Heddal (Telemark) and Urnes (Sognefjord).

# ROYALS ROM NEXT DOOR

Tall, dark and handsome Crown Prince Haakon is well known for his sporting achievements. In fact the entire Norwegian Royal House is down-to-earth, close to its people and above all sporty. The Crown Prince has been known to take part in the Birkebeiner race, a long-distance cross-country ski marathon held annually in Norway. King Harald (now 80) was an accomplished yachtsman, representing his country three times inthe Olympics. Every year the Royals also turn out to cheer on the ski jumpers at the Ski World Cup in Holmenkollen. Although she may not have won the hearts of Norwegians, Crown Princess Mette-Merrit has certainly gained their respect. Since her marriage to Prince Haakon, this former glamorous it-girl has earned a reputation in Europe as a befitting, if not slightly boring, princess. Her critics accuse her of being snobbish – a claim underpinned by sending her daughter Ingrid Alexandra to an exclusive private school in the west of Oslo rather than the local village school.

# B UORRE BEAIVI, OR GOOD DAY!

Red, blue, yellow, green – not a new traffic light system but the traditional colours of the only indigenous people in Europe. The Sami people are characterised by their colourful traditional costumes *(kofta)*, reindeers and *kohte*, or Sami huts, which attract thousands of visitors each year. The folkloric tradition generates a steady income but also reminds of the centuries of oppression. Today the Sami are committed to preserving their language and culture and represent their interests and rights in the Sameting, the advisory assembly in Karasjok. The traditional *joik* is a guttural form of yodelling, each emotionally driven song telling a story of ancient times and arduous living conditions in the harsh Nordic climate, their love of reindeers and their longing for recognition and independence.

# T HORN IN NORWAY'S SIDE

July 22, 2011: This date will be etched in every Norwegian's memory forever; the day when Anders Behring Breivik bombed Oslo's government buildings and then fired indiscriminately at youngsters taking part in a youth camp on the island of Utøya. 77 people were killed and this small country showed solidarity in its mourning for the victims who many knew personally or through friends by holding up roses as a symbol against Intolerance and xenophobia. The plans for a controversial memorial site to be erected on the island of Utøya, a clearly visible landmark when driving along the E16 from Oslo to Hønefoss, are still a matter of heated discussion. Imprisoned at the Telemark prison in Skien, the mass murderer still manages to hit the headlines, showing no signs of remorse or regret.

# I N BALANCE

Why is it that Scandinavia countries, including Norway, appear to have effortlessly achieved something what other nations have been struggling to get right for years? The work-life balance is based on the notion that tomorrow is another day and instead of living to work, the approach in Norway is much more that people work in order to live. Family and free time take a huge priority. The state endorses this view and promotes gender equality: both men and women have full-time jobs (working around 38 hours a week), are free to decide how they take their (well paid) parental leave and are guaranteed full-time childcare for their young ones from 18 months onwards. Norway has also established gender equality in the boardroom – it caused an international stir when it became the first country to enforce a mandatory female quota in its boardrooms.

# S KY PLAYING TRICKS

The phenomena known as the Northern Lights, or aurora borealis, take many a spectator by surprise. But be warned this celestial wonder carries a health warning with the potential risks being a stiff neck and heavy cold. Namely, the Northern Lights appear only at high latitudes on cold dark nights from September to March. But it's definitely worth the discomfort. Star-gazers can witness anything from an ethereal green glow or hazy white veil on the horizon to scarlet streaks across the sky. It is caused by the Earth's magnetic field drawing the sun's particles toward the poles, creating a breath-taking spectacle which leaves the audience speechless. So make yourself a hot flask of tea, wear your warmest clothes and let yourself be mesmerised by this natural phenomena.

## THE A-HA EFFECT

The Norwegian soul is a jukebox, serving up all kinds of great music in almost every genre. Remember "Take on me"? Then you were, or still are, a fan of the boy group A-ha, who enjoyed a string of hits in the 1980s. Since then others have taken their place in the pop music charts, including Madcon, Kygo or Nico & Vinz. Röyksopp is an experimental electronic music duo while Silje Nergaard has made a name for herself with her small-voiced jazz vocals. The most Norwegian of all the artists is Alexander Rybak who enjoyed a landslide victory at the 2009 Eurovision Song Contest 2009 with his song "Fairytale" playing the traditional Hardanger fiddle and performing the Halling dance. The celebrations were particularly memorable because his win luckily coincided with the country's National Holiday the next day.

## LONG LIVE THE DIALECT

Imagine if pupils in England had the subject dialect on their timetable as well as English. You may laugh but every Norwegian has to learn both Bokmål, a

written language similar to Danish, as well as Nynorsk, based on several different dialects. Children have to learn that "How are you?" can be expressed as either *Hvordan har du det?* or *Korleis har du det?* Although you will often hear

Celestial cinema in Kautokeino: the Northern Lights make you speechless

pupils complaining about the extra work, dialects are an important part of the Norwegian cultural identity and accepted in everyday life. Nobody would dream of switching to the more polished bokmål to improve understanding.

## LITERARY LIVES AND WORKS

When the Norwegians pack their suitcases for the Easter holidays to retreat to their cabins for a week of skiing and relaxation, they are sure to take the latest *påskekrim* (Easter crime fiction) with them. The author Jo Nesbø often releases one of his bestselling crime novels about his Oslo detective Harry Hole just in time for Easter. It's not surprising that Norwegians love a good read; they had to find some way to pass the time during the long winter months before the advent of the Internet and broadband. Over the years the country has also produced some of the most prolific writers and dramatists of contemporary social criticism. While Henrik Ibsen is linked to the birth of the modern drama in Europe, Knut Hamsun dedicated his book "Growth of the Soil" to the virtuosity of the farmers for which he was awarded the Nobel Prize for Literature in 1920. The most influential contemporary Norwegian writer today is Karl Ove Knausgård. His six-volume autobiographical work entitled "My Struggle" was ten years in the making and the hype surrounding his books is immense: in Norway alone they have sold half a million copies.

## SPECTACULAR COASTAL VOYAGE

If you prefer taking in scenery from the comfort of a deckchair and have the financial resources available, a cruise is a great way to explore Norway. In 2017, 110 cruise liners docked in the capital Oslo, transporting a total of 200,000 passengers. The most stunning of all the routes is the ● Hurtigruten (bookings at *www.hurtigruten.com)*. These postal ferry ships have been sailing between Bergen and Kirkenes since 1893 and not only transport passengers and vehicles but also supply food and provisions to Norway's coastal inhabitants. The ships sail along the rugged west coast, making ports of call along the way and even venturing into the Geirangerfjord past the Seven Sisters Waterfall, the best views of which can be had from the boat.

## SPIRIT OF ADVENTURE

It's a trait probably inherited by inhabitants of smaller countries and especially the descendants of the Vikings: They have an insatiable thirst for knowledge and curiosity to explore areas beyond their own borders. The zoologist and explorer Fridtjof Nansen set out to explore the North Pole on his boat called the *Fram*. Hard to believe today that the ship, which can be visited in the Oslo museum island Bygdøy, was trapped in pack ice for over three years. Roald Amundsen goes down in history

# NO. 1 IN ONE NIGHT STANDS

Yes, you have read it correctly! Who would have thought that these harmless, innocent Nordic people are in fact so promiscuous? Every third Norwegian practises "friendship one-night stands". To put it bluntly, Norway has become a world leader in casual sex. However this dubious reputation has a downside: in the throes of passion, contraception is all too readily forgotten. This is why the "after pill" is prescribed more often and sexually transmitted diseases are more common amongst Norwegians than their Nordic neighbours. According to surveys, the reason for this promiscuity lies in alcohol: Although Norwegians tend to go cold turkey during the week, they really let their hair down at weekends when the "drink till you drop" motto applies. "What actually happened last night?" is often a question to be heard the morning after.

Sailing through picture-book scenery: the MS Nordkapp ship along the Hurtigruten route

as the most successful polar explorer of all time, famous for beating Robert F. Scott in the race to the South Pole. The last in the line of famous Norwegian explorers is Thor Heyerdahl who built a raft, the *Kon-Tiki,* to cross the Pacific Ocean proving that people from South America had settled in Polynesia. The only thing missing is the first Norwegian astronaut...

## ON THE GREEN FAST LANE

Why do Norwegians always leave the light on? The fact is energy is a readily available and above all extremely cheap resource in Norway. Almost 99 percent of all electricity in Norway comes from hydropower thanks to the country's steep mountain slopes and abundance of water. In the past Norwegians have been accused of being wasteful and complacent about this copious supply, yet in times of climate change, attitudes are changing and the country has waged a war against the biggest cause of $CO_2$ pollution – the car. Norway is committed to what many call the "green shift" *(grønn skifte)* and is often heralded as a pioneer and role model by other countries. For a start, the government has banned diesel cars from driving in Oslo and plans to completely ban the sale of fossil fuel vehicles by 2025 and become a carbon-neutral society by 2030. Norwegian roads are filled with electric cars and for the drivers the motivation is less about climate protection and more about the financial benefits. Owners of electric cars are rewarded with a wide range of generous tax incentives and perks. Norwegians are just like us after all.

# FOOD & DRINK

**Think of Nordic food and images of mutton, dumplings and cabbage may spring to mind – but think again. Norway has reinvented its culinary identity thanks to influences from around the world, giving its traditional dishes a refined twist.**

There was a time in Norway when the waiter at the local Indian restaurant would ask you "How would you like your dish – Norwegian, medium or Indian hot?"– "Norwegian" stood for unseasoned and bland. It wasn't long ago that visitors were left feeling uninspired by Norwegian food, surviving off the stalwart pizza with a thick base and plenty of cheese or the traditional *kjøtt-kaker* or *karbonader* (meat balls) served with boiled potatoes and gravy.

Most of it was pretty bland stuff and it appeared that garlic had yet to cross the seas.

Norwegians then began to travel further afield and discover a taste for the exotic which they were keen to bring back home: alongside Thai, Vietnamese and Indian, *sushi* has become a firm favourite throughout this country of fish hlovers. Norwegian sushi is top-class, second in quality only to Japan (Japan also happens to be the largest importer of Norwegian fish). Not surprisingly really when you consider the abundance of fresh fish right on its doorstep. *Tacos* have replaced pizza as the regular family treat on Fridays. They are easy to make, healthy and children love them. *Pølse* (hotdogs), either in white buns

Photo: monkfish served at the Anno restaurant in Ålesund

**Tradition meets international fast food: it's quickly prepared meals that set the tone for everyday eating in Norway**

or lompe (a soft flatbread) are also readily available at every petrol station and kiosk.

On the subject of fast food: as most Norwegians work full time, elaborate cooking is usually reserved for national holidays or when friends come over to visit. Norwegians love to barbecue and will find any excuse to pull out their grill and throw on a *flintsteak,* a gigantic pork chop which could have been named after Fred Flintstone.

*Herrings (sild),* marinated in a variety of sauces, ranging from tomato, sherry, cream or mustard, are part of the staple diet and a convenient snack to stuff into your rucksack for a hike. Another classic dish is *makrell i tomat* (mackerel in tomato sauce) – no Norwegian breakfast would be complete without the iconic yellow tin from the Norwegian Stabburet brand. Another essential breakfast item is *brunost,* the traditional brown cheese with its unique malty taste. Try it for breakfast with a thin spreading of jam!

# LOCAL SPECIALITIES

**Eplekake med is** – warm apple cake with cinnamon and ice-cream

**Fiskekaker** – Fishcakes; eastern Norwegian variety: whitefish fillets mixed with potato flour, onions and salt and then formed into cakes and fried

**Klippfisk** – Dried cod, boiled and served with boiled potatoes, carrots, melted butter and parsley

**Kokt torsk** – Boiled cod, accompanied by carrots, boiled potatoes and melted butter (photo left)

**Lammesteik** – Roast lamb – a classic in autumn – seasoned with thyme, rosemary and garlic

**Lefse** – Flat pancakes made of sour cream, syrup, sugar, baking powder and wheat flour, served with sugar and butter

**Moltekrem** – Whipped cream mixed with cloudberry jam

**Ovnsbakt laks** – Salmon, stuffed with leek, celeriac and carrots, baked in the oven and seasoned with salt and garlic pepper

**Ovnsbakt steinbit** – Wolffish fillets baked in the oven, served with onions, apples and mushrooms fried in butter with apple juice and thyme

**Pasta med røkt laks** – Pasta with a sauce of onions and fish bouillon, cream and strips of (smoked) salmon or trout

**Raspeballer** – Potato dumplings with barley flour and diced bacon, served with puréed swedes and boiled potatoes. Accompanied by mutton or smoked sausage. In eastern Norway, this dish is called *komle*

**Røkt elgsteik** – Smoked elk meat, braised in the oven, with root vegetables, Brussels sprouts, game sauce and boiled potatoes

**Rømmegrøt** – Purée of sour cream, wheat flour or semolina and salt, refined with sugar and cinnamon. Salted meat is served as a side dish (photo right).

**Trollkrem** – Cranberries mixed with whipped egg whites, served cold

Since you're in the mood for experimenting with new tastes, the Norwegians also have some interesting (to say the least) festive dishes for you to try: Although rarely to be found on restaurant menus, a *sheep's head* (smalahove) or *cured lamb ribs* (pinnekjøtt) are traditionally served around Christmas time – the taste reminding you more of the dried twigs on which they are cooked rather than meat. Although the slimy consistency of *lutefisk* – dried cod soaked in brine and served with bacon and puréed peas – is not to everyone's taste, *rakørret* (trout soaked in brine for weeks and eaten with onions, cream and potatoes) is definitely worth a try. For a long time the Norwegians' national dish was *fårikål* – a stew of mutton in white cabbage – served especially in autumn.

Few Norwegian restaurants offer these home-cooked-style meals anymore due to a reinvention of Norwegian cuisine in line with contemporary tastes.

Vegetarian and vegan food is slow to take hold in a country which highly rates its quality of food and this includes its fish and meat.

*Popular snacks* on the menu are *rekesmør* (shrimps on bread), *skagenrøre* (bread with shrimps, crab and mussels in dill mayonnaise), fish soup or *blåskjell* (mussels).

Depending on the region and time of year, the *main meal* can include reindeer, elk or whale (for example whale carpaccio), all tastefully and artfully prepared. Although the rest of the world (except for Japan) shakes its head disapprovingly at the consumption of whale meat, Norwegians persist in hunting whales to seemingly prop up their national pride. You are advised not to enter into discussions on whaling if you're looking for new Norwegian friends and an objective take on the country.

Eating out is expensive and a luxury to be enjoyed once in a while. Excellentquality *wines* are available while Nordic *beer* tends to be on the bland side. Bread, butter and cold tap water are all served to the table without a surcharge. Norwegians like to finish their meal with a *filter coffee*, a popular

A breakfast speciality: the brown *brunost* cheese

beverage to be drunk at any time of the day. With a per capita consumption of 10 kg/22 lbs per year, Norway is topped only by Finland in the world's top coffee consuming nations.

A fatty meal is often digested with a glass of *linie aquavit* named after the tradition of sending barrels of aquavit on a sea journey across the world to mature, crossing the Equator twice to gain its unique taste.

# SHOPPING

There are three things that make shopping in Norway a truly enjoyable experience: excellent quality, Scandinavian taste in design and that certain "je ne sais quoi" which makes your holiday souvenir that little bit special. Although shopping in Norway never comes cheap with a 25% VAT rate, authentic, made in Norway clothing, jewellery and interior items are timeless pieces, incorporating an element of Nordic spirit in each one. Traditional Norwegian arts and crafts can be found in the *Husflid* stores *(norskflid.no)* dotted all over the country. A wide selection of high-quality souvenirs are waiting to be found – ranging from woollen gloves and cuddly blankets to silver jewellery.

## CLOTHING & ACCESSORIES

Look out for signs showing *tilbud* – bargains with reductions of up to 70 percent can often be found. Clothes designed by *Moods of Norway (moodsofnorway.com)*, the clothing brand with the pink tractor, have reached an almost cult status. Less well-known, perhaps, yet stylish, eccentric and urban is the clothing from Oslo designer *Tulip & Tatamo (tulipogtatamo. no)*. The original idea for *Swims (swims. com)* came from Bergen (where else?).

They are a contemporary take on the traditional galoshes – very popular with business people who want to protect their leather shoes from the rain. The rain coats and outerwear by *Norwegian Rain (norwegianrain.com)* also come from Bergen. Fashionista, Crown Princess Mette-Marit, wears clothes designed by the young fashion label *FWSS (Fall Winter Spring Summer) (fwss.com)*.

## INTERIOR ITEMS & CHEESE SLICERS

Norwegian product designers are full of quirky ideas; a good choice of their modern creations can be found at *Purnorsk (www.purnorsk.no)* in Oslo or online. How about an oil rig made of wooden building bricks for children? Or a lamp in the shape of a speech bubble from *Northern Lighting?* If you don't have a lot of space in your suitcase, then go for one of Norway's best export products and inventions, a steel or silver cheese slicer with a prettily decorated handle.

## KNITWEAR

Looking for the quintessential Norwegian souvenir? Then look no further than a

## From reindeer skin to quirky designer items: between extremes, the perfect souvenir is just waiting to be found

traditional pullover – a timeless, high-quality item of clothing available from *Dale of Norway (daleofnorway.com)* or *Devold (devold.no)*. Both ☺ *Janus (janus.no)* and ☺ *Ulvang (ulvang.no)* special-isein ecological and versatile knitwear. *Nøstebarn (nostebarn.no)* sells cuddly children clothing from untreated wool. **INSIDER TIP** *Oleana (oleana.no)* from Bergen is famous for its beautiful and colourful items of knitwear, inspired by the roses, leaves and vines adorning ancient fishing boats.

### SMOKED SALMON & CO.

You can recognise good smoked salmon by its darker colour; it is dryer and smells more strongly of smoke than lower quality fish. Generally speaking, less salt means more taste. Try the salmon before you buy it. Shrink-wrapped salmon from the supermarket can also be good quality, but pay attention to its colour. You can almost taste Norway's rugged coast

in a tube of caviar ideal as a sandwich spread. *Den blinde Ku* – the blind cow –, cheese with a one-eyed cow as its logo, is a cult dairy product and an insider tip among cheese lovers.

### SPORTS & OUTDOOR GEAR

Anybody who has hiked in a Norwegian fjell knows what you need. Everything must be of the highest quality and ready for whatever Mother Nature brings. *Bergans (www.bergans.com)* is a "genuine Norwegian" producer, offering premium quality rucksacks and tents since 1908. The former freestyle skier *Kari Traa (karitraa.com)* makes universal sportswear for women. *Hellyhansen (hellyhansen.com)* is a major name among sailors and yachtsmen. *Odlo (odlo.no)* produces fashionable and sustainable ski underwear and performance clothing just as *Norrøna (norrona.no)* whose brightly coloured ski jackets and trousers set the trend on Europe's ski slopes.

# THE SOUTH

Emerging from cool mountain lakes, raging rivers force their way through dense forests. Bays lie hidden along the coast with its countless skerries, shiny washed boulders and ports that have preserved the charm of the steamship age.

Swimming in water that is above 20°C (68°F) warm is just one of the many attractions of a summer holiday in Sørlandet, the coastal strip along the Skagerrak. There are plenty of beaches with shallow water and moorings but the really peaceful places are far from the coastal towns. Although southern Norway is a destination for water sports enthusiasts, it is also popular with hikers, for the fjell – the long expanse of high hills –, in spite of only being sparsely covered with vegeta-

tion, provides a foretaste of the amazingly rich arctic fauna and flora. The south of Norway is full of rich colour and varying landscapes, and it isn't cold by any means.

# FREDRIKSTAD

(137 E5) *(ɒɒ D17)* **Once you arrive, you'll never want to leave: Situated in the far south of Norway and 40 km/25 miles from the Swedish border, the idyllic town of Fredrikstad is like a step back in time.** The town's pretty and historic charm keeps you captivated and longing to stay in this by-gone era. This former garrison town (pop. 80,000) remains an insider tip among tourists and the surrounding

Urban Norway and the wilderness beyond: charming places and verdant nature hidden between islands and skerries

region also has lots to offer: Norway's longest river, the Glomma, flows into the town from the north east and merges into the Oslofjord upon leaving.

## SIGHTSEEING

### FREDRIKSTAD DOMKIRKE (CATHEDRAL)

The best time to visit this neo-Gothic church dating from 1880 is at night: the steeple contains a lighthouse, which still functions at night. Those visiting by day should go inside to admire the stained glass work by Emanuel Vigeland. *Tue–Thu 11am–1pm | Nygaardsgata 6*

### FREDRIKSTAD MUSEUM

It is not clear where the museum stops and the *Bar 1567* starts – a conscious decision by the curators and which makes this museum all the more exciting. Take a trip back through the history of Fredrikstad accompanied by music, theatre and dance and explore a different side to this charming city. *23 June–1 Oct daily*

Monument to commemorate Frederick II, the founder after whom the city is named

*noon– 4pm | admission 75 NOK | Tøihusgaten 41 | ostfoldmuseene.no*

### GAMLEBYEN (FORT AND OLD TOWN)

Since it was founded in 1567, the old town has lost little of its charm. Take time out to wander through the many galleries and art and craft shops. Small restaurants and coffee shops such as *Café Magenta* in Bastion 5 serve refreshing beverages and snacks for a deserved break.

## FOOD & DRINK

### MAJOREN STUE & KRO

Travel back to garrison times: the authentic *majorens viltburger* fits perfectly with the historic ambience. *Voldportgaten 73 | tel. 69 32 15 55 | www.majoren.no | Expensive*

### MORMORS CAFÉ ✪

Organic dishes are made to order at this café/restaurant in the old town centre. The bread is always fresh, the perfect basis for the tasty delicacies like roast beef sandwich with truffle aioli and parmesan cheese. *Raadhusgaten 18a | tel. 69 32 16 60 | www. mormorscafe.com | Moderate*

## SHOPPING

### GLASHYTTA

The products made by the Kenyan glass artist Abel Sawe are characterised by their strong colours and unusual forms. There is a small museum and shop. *Mon–Fri 8am–4pm, Sat 11am–3pm | Tornesveien 1 | Gamlebyen | www.fredrikstadoghvaler. no/glasshyttao*

## WHERE TO STAY

### HANKØ FJORDHOTELL & SPA

Here, pure relaxation is top priority. Swimming pool, tennis court, fitness room and a spacious spa area, surrounded by magnificent countryside with forests on the banks of the fjord. *102 rooms | Hankø | tel. 69 38 28 50 | www.hankoh otell.no | Expensive*

## INFORMATION

*Turistkontor (Kirkegaten 31B | tel. 69 30 46 00 | www.visitoestfold.com)*

## WHERE TO GO

### HVALER (137 E5) (*D17*)

An island hopping adventure. The municipality of Hvaler is a group of 833 islands, holms and islets. Landlubbers can explore this picture-book region by taking a boat trip *(55 NOK | tel. 90 85 71 21 | www. visitoestfold.com)* which docks at several picturesque beaches along the way including INSIDERTIP *Kirkeøy* in the far south. The tour starts in the main centre of Skjærhalden (25 km/15 miles south of Fredrikstad).

# JOTUN-HEIMEN

**(136 C1–2) (*C14*) Translated literally, Jotunheimen means "homeland of the giants". It is Norway's only high mountain range, making it a popular destination for hikers, mountaineers and skiers.** Here, a chain of mountains over 2,000 m (6,600 ft) high stretches out one after the other, some of them crowned with glaciers. However, even the highest of them, Galdhøpiggen – at 2,469 m (8,100 ft) the highest mountain in Norway and all of Scandinavia – can be climbed by children.

## SIGHTSEEING

### GALDHØPIGGEN

Norway's highest peak is accessible to even children and dogs. All you need is good waterproof outdoor clothing and a dog that can withstand a storm or hailstones as the weather is known to be extremely variable. For the 15 km/9 mile guided tour *(May–Oct daily from 10am | 250 NOK | starts from Juvasshytta)* you should expect to take six to seven hours there and back.

INSIDERTIP **KLIMAPARK 2469**

Nobody will laugh at you for wearing a hat and gloves here in the middle of summer. On the contrary, you'll be well prepared to go 60 m/200 feet down into the solid ice below you. The guided tour takes you on a hike through the climate park followed by a 400 m/1310 ft long ice tunnel underneath Galdhøpiggen Mountain. The ice cave also contains bows and arrows, pitfalls and tools of the first cave inhabitants and tracks the climate changes over the last 6000 years. *Guided tours end of June–end of August, daily at 10:30am and 2pm from the Juvasshytta mountain hut | 345 NOK (including admission to Norsk Fjellsenter) | klimapark2469.no*

**NORSK FJELLSENTER** ●

A good address for providing excellent tour information. In the museum next door, discover how this barren region with its harsh winters and short summers affected the lives of its inhabitants. *15 May–25 June, 21 Aug–8 Oct Mon–Fri 9am–4pm, Sat/Sun 9am–3pm, 26 June–20 Aug until 7pm/5pm | admission 80 NOK | Brubakken 2 | www.norskfjellsenter.no*

**SOGNEFJELLSVEI**

Road 55 from Lom to Skjolden is a landscaped scenic route and runs through icy heights. With a place to stop for a rest at 1,400 m (4,600 ft), glacier snouts, hiking trails and places to fish to the left and right of the road the journey is an eventful encounter with the Norwegian mountain world. *www.nasjonaleturistveger.no*

## FOOD & DRINK

**INSIDER TIP** BAKERIET I LOM ☺

Master chef Morten Schakenda studied all the finer points of the baker's art and in 2004 opened a bakery and slow-food café at the Prestefosse waterfall in Lom – a joy for all the senses. *www.bakerietilom.no*

## WHERE TO STAY

**BØVERDALEN VANDRERHJEM**

One of the prettiest youth hostels in the country judging on the basis of location. Situated 18 km/11 miles from Lom with almost two dozen peaks over 2,000 m (6,561 ft) nearby and plenty of activities (cycling!). *7 rooms (32 beds), several huts | Sognefjellsveien 1931 | on Road 55 | tel. 61 21 20064 | www.hihostels.no | Budget*

**STORHAUGEN GÅRD** ☣

This farm is situated at a height of 800 m (2,600 ft) with a view of mountain peaks. Flats in the main house or in the neighbouring cabins with at least 5 beds; everything is simple but well cared-for. You can even help out on the farm. E-mail reservations preferred. *70 beds | near Galdesand on Road 55 | tel. 9110 89 42 | www.storhaugengard.no | info@storhaugengard.no | Budget–Moderate*

## INFORMATION

*Turistinformasjon (Sognefjellsvegen 17 | Lom | tel. 61 21 29 90 | www.visitjotunheimen.com)*

# KRISTIAN-SAND

**(136 C6)** *(∅ B18)* **A light summer dress and shorts in Norway? If not in Kristiansand, then nowhere else.**

This harbour city (pop. 86,000) is regarded as the country's warmest spot with white sandy beaches and optimal sailing conditions between the offshore

## LOW BUDGET

You can often eat for less than 120 NOK in the multiculti districts of Oslo – and right at Frognerparken at *Curry & Ketchup (Kirkeveien 51 | tel. 22 69 05 22).*

At *Haraldsheim Vandrerhjem (88 rooms | Haraldsheimveien 4 | 4 km (2½ miles) from the city centre | tel. 22 22 29 65 | www.harladsheim.no)* in Oslo, the cheapest bed costs 260 NOK per night.

Kristiansand: Norway's sunnier side

islets and is a great place to relax. The range of activities for families, sun worshippers and water sports enthusiasts is second to none thanks to the beautiful skerry landscape on the Skagerrak. Not surprising that the Royals have their summer residence in Kristiansand. The right-angled layout of the streets was ordered by the Danish-Norwegian King Christian IV who established the town on a sandy promontory in 1641.

## SIGHTSEEING

### KRISTIANSAND MUSEUM
Open-air museum housing 40 historic buildings in total. You can visit workshops, a small grocer's shop as well as a miniature model town where you suddenly feel like Gulliver. *20 June–20 Aug Mon–Fri 10am–5pm, Sat/Sun noon–5pm | admission 90 NOK | Vigeveien 22B | www.vest agdermuseet.no*

### SØRLANDETS KUNSTMUSEUM
The exhibitions in the contemporary-designed light rooms present local art from the last 300 years. Some of the works portray the harsh lives of their painters. The coffee shop offers views of the surrounding area. *Tue–Sat 11am–5pm, Sun noon–4pm | admission 80 NOK | Skippergata 24 B | www.skmu.no*

## FOOD & DRINK

### BAKGÅRDEN BAR & RESTAURANT
Locals love their inspiring and creative menu. Afterwards head to the bar which serves the town's finest cocktails, all of which can be ordered without alcohol for non-drinkers. *Tollbodgata 5A | tel. 38 02 12 11 | www.bakgardenbar.no | Moderate–Expensive*

## SHOPPING

*Kvadraturen*, which refers to the right-angled layout of the town centre, is an ideal place to take a stroll. There are many small shops, cafés and restaurants. *Hansen & Co (Skippergata 14 | hansenco. no)* sells Scandinavian interior design from functional to ...just great! A break from shopping with a perfect latte macchiato: at the tiny *Cuba Life* cafe *(Tollbodgata 6).*

## BEACHES

(136 C6) (*∅ B–C18*) Typical places for swimming are small oases of sand between the boulders on the shore. Large sandy beaches: *Bertnes Bay* (3 km/1¾ mile east) and *Hamresanden* (11 km/6¾ miles east). These, along with *Bystranda* in Kristiansand and *Skotteviga* near Lillesand (31 km/19¼ miles to the east), are among the cleanest beaches in southern Norway.

Sea view for over 100 years: lighthouse at Cape Lindesnes

## WHERE TO STAY

INSIDER TIP  YESS! HOTEL

For families and young people between the centre of town and the ferry port; very small rooms (but good mattresses!); the evening and breakfast buffets are full of surprises like homemade pizza or tapas. *55 rooms | Tordenskjoldsgate 12 | tel. 38 70 15 70 | www.yesshotel.no | Budget*

## INFORMATION

*Kristiansand Turistkontor (Rådhusgate 18 | tel. 38 07 50 00 | www.visitkrs.no)*

## WHERE TO GO

CAPE LINDESNES ⚓ (136 B6) (*∅ B18*)
The lighthouse on Norway's southern cape, built in 1915, stands on a small hill 80 km/50 miles to the west of Kristiansand. The *Lighthouse Museum (in summer daily 10am–8pm, other seasons until 5pm | admission 75 NOK | www.lindesnesffyr.no)*, built by blasting away the rock, is well worth a visit.

### MANDAL (136 C6) (*∅ B18*)

This once important seafaring town (pop. 10,500) with pretty wooden houses in its centre, lies at the mouth of the River Mandalselva. If the weather is fine in summer, make sure to visit one of the many city beaches. Wool is still washed, woven and spun in the woollen factory *Sjølingstad Uldvarefabrik* that was opened in 1894 *(in summer daily 11am–5pm | tours by appointment at 11am, 1pm and 3pm, museum shop Mon–Fri 11am–3pm | www.vestagdermuseet.no/sjolingstad | around 8 km/5 miles to the west of Mandal, turn off the E 39). www.lindesnesregionen.com | 41 km/25½ miles west of Kristiansand*

### RISØR ★ (137 D5) (*∅ C17–18*)

The "white town on the Skaggerak" (pop. 4,500) with wonderful areas of wooden houses and impressive patrician residences along the harbour promenade is the most important gathering place for wooden-boat fans (festival beginning of August). A fun place is the aquarium with its *underwater post office (July–1 Sept Wed, Sat | Strandgata 14 | information at Tore Bjørn Hovde | tel. 91 57 13 12)*, where you can have your letters and postcards stamped. *Risør Resort Moen Camping (tel. 37 15 50 91 | www.moen camping.no | Moderate)*, with cabins and flats, camping site and beach, is only 10 km/6¼ miles from the centre of town. *www.risor.no | 116 km/72 miles north-east of Kristiansand*

# LILLE-HAMMER

**(137 E2)** *(ⓜ D15)* **Ever dreamt of how it felt to be a ski jumper at the 1994 Winter Olympics?**

Then head straight to the ski jumping centre *Lysgårdsbakken* in Lillehammer (pop. 28,000) *(3 June–13 Aug daily 9am–7pm, shorter opening times in other months | admission 25 NOK | Birkebeinervegen 122 | www.olympiaparken.no).* From the top of the ⛷ ski jump, you have amazing panoramic views of the city over to the Mjøsa Lake, Norway's largest inland lake. If you're not prepared to walk up the 936 steps to get there, the chairlift will take you up and down for 60 NOK.

## SIGHTSEEING

### MAIHAUGEN

Lillehammer is the gateway to Gudbrandsdalen. More than 170 buildings will not only give you an idea of the rural culture of the valley but also of craftsmanship from all over Norway. Many of the workshops are still in use. Changing exhibitions. *Mid-June–mid Aug daily 10am–5pm, otherwise shorter opening hours | admission 170 NOK | www.maihaugen.no*

### NORGES OLYMPISKE MUSEUM

This museum is dedicated to Norway's main national sport. If you share the Norwegians' passion for skiing, you are sure to love this homage to the legendary Winter Olympics held in Norway in 1952 and 1994. Cheering crowds and glorious winners – the multimedia presentations are sure to set your pulse racing. *June–Aug daily 10am–5pm, otherwise Tue–Sun 11am–4pm | admission 130 NOK | Maihaugvegen 1 | www.maihaugen.no*

## FOOD & DRINK

**INSIDER TIP ATELIER KAKAO**

Fresh olive bread, pasta salads and yummy cakes (including Austrian Sachertorte!) plus very fine chocolate creations are served up in this café with *chocolaterie. Storgata 48*

### BLÅMANN RESTAURANT & BAR

First-class lunch dishes from north, south, west and east in the centre of town. The hamburger variations are popular and quite filling! *Lilletorvet 1 | tel. 61 26 22 03 | www.blaamann.com | Moderate*

## SHOPPING

### JANUS FABRIKKBUTIKK

Traditional ski underwear from Janus comes from Espeland near Bergen. This store is one of four factory outlets in Norway. These traditional Norwegian fleece garments keep you so warm that you'll want to take a set back home. *Storgata 45*

## WHERE TO STAY

### BIRKEBEINEREN HOTEL & APARTMENTS

On a slope between the ski jump and the city, the atmosphere is somewhere between that of a hotel and fjell guesthouse. From toddler to teen – no one will get bored. Good service, too. *54 rooms, 40 apartments | Birkebeinervegen 24 | tel. 61 05 00 80 | www.birkebeineren.no | Moderate*

### LILLEHAMMER VANDRERHJERN STASJONEN

Simple, good hostel right inside the station, has some five-bed dorms. Towels, bed linens and breakfast included. Buses go to the Hafjell and Nordseter ski areas. *29 rooms (80 beds) | Jernbanetorget 2 |*

*in train station | tel. 61 26 00 24 | www.
stasjonen.no | Budget*

### INFORMATION

*Turistkontor (Jernbanetoget 2 | tel.
61 28 98 00 | www.lillehammer.com)*

under a gigantic glass pyramid and you
can stay dry while learning more about
this former religious centre in Norway.
You will need better weather though if
you are to explore the 65 buildings in the
*Hedmark outdoor museum* next door and
to enjoy a picnic on the banks of the de-

Put your hiking boots on and hike through Rondane National Park with its autumn colours

### WHERE TO GO

#### AULESTAD (137 D2) *(⚏ D15)*
Blueberry pancakes were the favourite
food of the Norwegian national poet
Bjørnstjerne Bjørnson. It's worth taking
a detour to his residence if alone for its
idyllic setting: time seems to have stood
still in his lovingly preserved house and
the *Drengestua* (servant's quarters) café
serves delicious pancakes. *May–Aug dai-
ly 10am–5pm | admission 130 NOK | Aul-
estadvegen 6–14 | Follebu | aulestad.no |
18 km/11 miles northwest of Lillehammer*

#### HAMAR (137 E2) *(⚏ D15)*
Surprisingly, Hamar (pop. 31,000) is the
place to visit on rainy days because the
● *ruins of the cathedral* and the partially
excavated *bishop's palace* are preserved

lightful Mjøsa Lake. Fingers crossed. *21
May–18 June, 14 Aug–3 Sept Tue–Sun
10am–4pm, 19 June–13 Aug daily 10am–
5pm | admission ruins and museum 110
NOK | Strandvegen 100 | domkirkeodden.
no | Information: Hamar Turistkontor
(Grönnegata 52 | tel. 40 03 60 36 | www.
visit-hedmark.no/en/hamar-region) | 60
km/37 miles southeast of Lillehammer*

#### PEER-GYNT-VEIEN ☀
#### (137 D1–2) *(⚏ C–D 14–15)*
This splendid 60 km/37 miles long mountain road takes you to heights of more
than 1,000 m/3,300 ft. Take a break
along the way to soak in the magnificent
view of the Jotunheimen, Rondane and
Dovrefjell Mountains. Elks can be spotted
here until well into autumn (guided safari tours in Gålå) and you can spend

hours here fishing for freshwater trout, hiking through this beautiful region and enjoying a break at the *Fagerhøy Alm (www.fagerhoi.no)*. The road also attracts cyclists. The ● *Peer Gynt Festival (tickets from 175 NOK | www.peergynt.no)* takes place here every year at the start of August. Henrik Ibsen's famous play is performed against the absolutely beautiful scenery of Lake Gålåvanet accompanied by the music composed by Edvard Grieg. *Toll station (150 NOK one way) | www.peergyntvegen.no*

### RONDANE NATIONAL PARK ⤳
### (137 D1) *(ᗰ C–D14)*

*Back to nature* is the motto in this 964 km²/600 miles² National Park which also welcomes camper vans. Standing an impressive 10 m/32 ft high, the world's largest elk sculpture greets drivers at the parking area at *Bjøråa* (137 E1) *(ᗰ D14)*. Stretching out over Gudbrandsdalen, Dovrefjell, Jotunheimen and Rondane, the region is home to Norway's highest mountains, making it a paradise for recreational pursuits including hiking, fishing, rafting and ski mountaineering – you can however relax with a spot of animal watching or a massage for aching muscles at the spa in the *Rondane Høyfjellshotell (50 rooms, 10 huts | turnoff from the E 6 near Odda | tel. 61 20 90 90 | www.rondane.no | Budget–Expensive)*. *www.nasjonalparkriket.no*

# OSLO

⬛ MAP INSIDE BACK COVER
⬛ (137 E4) *(ᗰ D16)* **The small capital city with a vast hinterland: Norway's metropolis (pop. 670,000) at the foot of the Oslofjord climbs up the slopes of the wooded Nordmarka.**

Oslo first became the seat of the Norwegian royal family under King Håkon V (1299–1319). The town was called Christiania from the 14th to the beginning of the 19th century when Norway was still part of Denmark and it was overshadowed by Copenhagen, Bergen and Trondheim. It only started to flourish again at the end of the 19th century and in 1925 it was given its old name once more.

You definitely should visit the historic district of Oslo near Akershus Fortress. The "citizen's quarter" near Frognerparken and the multicultural Grønland suburb to the east of the main station are also well worth seeing. Oslo's smart shopping street Karl Johans gate stretches from the railway station to the Royal Palace – the ⤳ palace square offers one of the prettiest views in the city. With the *Oslo Pass (24 hours 395 NOK, 48 hours 595 NOK, 72 hours 745 NOK | www.visitoslo.com)* you can travel by bus and train free of charge and visit most of the main sights. More detailed information can be found in the MARCO POLO travel guide for Oslo.

## SIGHTSEEING

### AKERSHUS FESTNING OG SLOTT
### (U D–E 5–6) *(ᗰ d–e 5–6)*

One of the most important medieval buildings in Norway lies on a promontory jutting out into the Oslofjord. Akershus was a fortress from 1319 to 1380 and transformed into a *castle* by King Christian IV at the beginning of the 17th century. Today, it is used for state receptions while the ● ⤳ fortress complex is a favourite place for sun worshippers. *Fortress complex daily 6am–9pm | free admission | castle (with royal mausoleum) mid-June–Aug Mon–Sat 10am–4pm, Sun noon–4pm | admission 100 NOK*

### ASTRUP FEARNLEY MUSEET ★
(U C5) (🗺 c5)

Oslo's newest architectural masterpiece is situated directly on the fjord. The collection of this museum on the Tjuvholmen promontory includes works by Damien Hirst, Andy Warhol, Jeff Koons and Anselm Kiefer. Just a stroll through the steel and glass buildings designed by Renzo Piano topped by a "sail" is an experience in and of itself, and the temporary exhibits are excellent. *Tue–Fri noon–5pm (Thu until 7pm), Sat/Sun 11am–5pm | admission 120 NOK | Strandpromenaden 2 | www.afmuseet.no*

---

🏙 **WHERE TO START?**
**Operahuset (U F5)** *(🗺 f5)*: The Opera House is the perfect starting point as it is located both directly on the fjord and opposite the main station. Drive to one of the many multi-storey car parks near the railway station, walk across to the opera house and plan your stroll through the city from its accessible rooftop.

---

### HENIE-ONSTAD-KUNSTSENTER
(0) (🗺 0)

Housing over 4000 paintings, this art centre boasts one of the largest collections of contemporary art in Scandinavia. Some of the artists are only known in artistic circles but there are other more accomplished names such as Kurt Schwitters or Victor Vasarely. *Tue–Sun 11am–5pm | admission 100 NOK | www.hok.no | Høvikodden (12 km/7½ miles west of Oslo), motorway to Drammen/Bærum exit*

### HOLMENKOLLEN ★ ● ⛷ (0) (🗺 0)

The "mecca for Norwegian skiers" is dominated by the extremely modern main ski jump that was opened in 2010. The view of the city, the fjord and the forests in the area is breathtaking. If you come here, you should also visit the *Ski Museum (June–Aug daily 9am–8pm, May/Sept 10am–5pm, otherwise 10am–4pm | admission 130 NOK | www.holmenkollen.com | 8 km/5 miles northwest of the city centre | Holmenkollen train from Majorstuen Station*

### IBSENMUSEET (U C4) (🗺 c4)

"Eternally owned is but what's lost" is just one of 69 quotes embedded in the pavement where Henrik Ibsen once walked every day. The trail of quotes starts at his apartment in Arbins gate, today a lovingly designed museum in memory of this great writer and poet. *15 May–14 Sept daily 10am–6pm, otherwise Fri–Wed 11am–4pm, Thu until 6pm | admission including tour 115 NOK | Henrik Ibsens gate 26 | www.ibsenmuseet.no*

### MUNCHMUSEET (0) (🗺 0)

The gift of the famous Norwegian artist Edvard Munch (1863–1944) to his home town: around 1,100 paintings, along with thousands of drawings and watercolours, graphic works and correspondence. *Early May–early Oct daily 10am–5pm, otherwise until 4pm | admission 100 NOK | Tøyengata 53 | www.munchmuseet.no*

### BYGDØY MUSEUM ISLAND
(U A6) (🗺 a6)

The ideal destination to get your first impressions of Norway's history and culture. The *Fram-Museet (summer daily 9am–6pm, otherwise shorter opening hours | admission 100 NOK | www.frammuseum.no)* is devoted to a single ship. Built in 1892, the three-masted *Fram* (Forwards) was the expedition ship in which Fridtjof Nansen, Otto Sverdrup and Roald Amundsen set sail for the Arctic and

Antarctic. You can see the adventurer and researcher Thor Heyerdahl's Kon-Tiki raft, the papyrus boat Ra II and a model of the Tigris in the *Kon-Tiki-Museum (in summer daily 9:30am–6pm, otherwise shorter opening hours | admission 100 NOK | www. kon-tiki.no)*.

*Gjøa*, the yacht Roald Amundsen used to sail around North America between 1903 and 1905 belongs to the collection of the *Norsk Maritimt Museum (mid-May–Sept daily 10am–5pm, otherwise shorter opening hours | admission 100 NOK | www. marmuseum.no)*. Three Viking ships that were found in burial mounds on the Oslofjord (especially impressive: the *Oseberg Ship*) can be seen in the *Vikingskipshuset (May–Sept daily 9am–6pm, otherwise shorter opening hours | admission 100 NOK | www.khm.uio.no)*.

170 houses have been rebuilt in the *Norsk Folkemuseum (mid-May–mid-Sept daily 10am–6pm, otherwise shorter opening hours | admission 130 NOK | www.norsk folkemuseum.no)* to show how life was lived in Norway over the centuries. The oldest building is the *stave church from Gol* (around 1200).

## NASJONALGALLERIET ⭐ (U D4) (𝄐 d4)

The museum's holdings include 4,500 paintings, 1,500 sculptures and more than 40,000 drawings and pieces of graphic art. Works by Edvard Munch are on display along with the main "Norwegian National Romanticism" exhibits. Temporary exhibitions of an international standard are held. *Tue–Fri 10am–6pm (Thu until 7pm), Sat/ Sun 11am–5pm | free admission on Thu, otherwise 100 NOK | Universitetsgata 13 | www.nasjonalmuseet.no*

## OPERAHUSET ⭐
(U F5) (𝄐 f5)

The award-winning opera house on Bjørvika Bay is an Oslo landmark: white marble, lots of glass, a magnificent interior and a roof with a 🔆 panoramic view

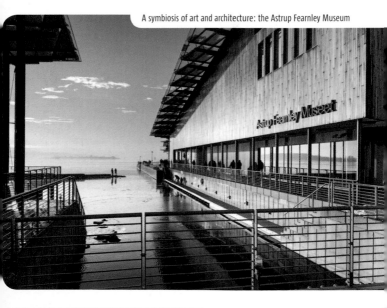
A symbiosis of art and architecture: the Astrup Fearnley Museum

Inside the music, outside the skies above: the roof of the Oslo Opera House

open to the public – a wonderful experience regardless of the weather. *Tours in English daily in summer at 11am, noon, 1pm and 3 pm | admission 100 NOK | www. operaen.no*

### RÅDHUSET ● (U D4) (*ⅅ d4*)

With its two towers, the red-brick town hall built between 1930 and 1955 stands like a mighty gate between the harbour and inner city. Inside, you can see monumental paintings including works by Edvard Munch. *Daily 9am–6pm | free admission*

### VIGELANDSPARKEN ●
(U A1–2) (*ⅅ a1–2*)

The complex with around 200 sculptures by Gustav Vigeland is just one section of the vast Frognerpark that is especially popular in summer. You should take your time walking up the avenue of stones leading to the 17 m/56 ft ⚡ *Monolitten* and take in the aura of the figures that depict the cycle of life. From the upper end, you have a great view over the park and suburb of Frogner all the way to the

city centre. *Open 24 hours a day | free admission | main entrance Kirkeveien | www.vigelandmuseum.no*

### THE BROKER (U C1) (*ⅅ c1*)

Best hamburgers in town and perfectly tapped beer. *Bogstadveien 27 | tel. 22 60 34 80 | www.thebroker.no | Budget*

### INSIDER TIP CAFÉ LAUNDROMAT
(U D2) (*ⅅ d2*)

A home from home where you can spend your time eating and reading while doing your laundry. The originally named burgers (such as *Lucky Bastard)* are deliciously succulent, breakfast is served until 5pm. Close to the university, with a living room setting. *Underhaugsveien 2 | tel. 21 38 36 29 | www.laundromat.no | Moderate*

### SMALHANS (U E2) (*ⅅ e2*)

Casual atmosphere with a concept to match its clientele. Order lunch at the bar (until 4pm) and put together your own menu at your table after 6pm. A dish of the day is offered in between. *Waldemar Thranesgate 10 | enter on Ullevålsveien | tel. 22 69 60 00 | www.smalhans.no | Expensive*

### VILLA PARADISO (U F2) *(ᶆ f2)*

Oslo's best pizza, baked in a stone oven from Naples. *Olav Ryes plass 8 | tel. 22 35 40 60 | www.villaparadiso.no | Budget*

## SHOPPING

Your stroll begins on *Karl Johans gate* (U D–E4) *(ᶆ d–e4)* where international labels have their shops. For more relaxed shopping, head to *Steen & Strøm (Nedre Slottsgate, at right angles to Karl Johan)* and *Paleet (Karl Johans gate 37)*. The ◍ *Mathallen (market hall)* (U F2) *(ᶆ f2) (Closed Mon | Vulkan 5)* with its stalls and shops plus restaurants, bistros and snack bars is a paradise for food-lovers. Organic products from all over Norway, ranging from seafood delicacies to sausages and cheese. ◍*Godtbrød* (U F2 *(ᶆ f2) (Thorvald Meyers Gate 49)* bakes bread and cakes using only organic ingredients. The *skillingsboller* sprinkled with cinnamon and sugar are especially tasty.

## SPORTS & ACTIVITIES

Visitors to Oslo who want to see fjord and fjell landscapes should make an excursion to *Nordmarka* (0) *(ᶆ 0)*. This recreation area starts at the Holmenkollen Ski Centre and offers 2,600 km/1,600 miles of prepared cross-county trails where skiers and hikers can either stay overnight in cabins or just come for the day.

## ENTERTAINMENT

A stroll along fashionable *Aker Brygge* (U C5) *(ᶆ c5)*, in the *Frognerpark* (U A1–2) *(ᶆ a1–2)* or to Akershus Fortress is especially enjoyable on a summer evening. There are many café/clubs in *Grønland* (0) *(ᶆ 0)* and *Grünerløkka* (U F2–3) *(ᶆ f2–3)* that serve Italian coffee in the afternoon, play rock music in the early evening and funk late at night. *Bare Jazz* (U E4) *(ᶆ e4) (Grensen 8 | www.barejazz. no)* is a music shop, café and concert venue all rolled into one that attracts jazz fans from around the world. A boat hangs from the ceiling of the **INSIDER TIP** *Aku-Aku Tiki Bar* (U F2) *(ᶆ f2) (Thorvald Meyers gate 32 | www.akuaku.no)* – maybe as a homage to Thor Heyerdahl after whose book this bar is named. This Polynesian-inspired bar also serves great cocktails.

## WHERE TO STAY

### COCHS PENSJONAT (U C3) *(ᶆ c3)*

Traditional family business near the palace park, only a few minutes away from the palace itself. *88 rooms | Parkveien 25 | tel. 23 33 24 00 | www.cochspensjonat. no | Moderate*

### HOLLMENKOLLEN PARK HOTEL ● ⊰⊱ (0) *(ᶆ 0)*

Heads of state are regular guests at this hotel – a wooden fairy-tale castle that is a Swiss-style architectural gem decorated with dragon heads. There is a view over the city from the veranda. Furnishings, service and restaurant, everything is the best. The spa adds the finishing touch to the perfect hotel experience. *336 rooms | Kongeveien 26 | tel. 22 92 20 00 | www. hollmenkollenparkhotel.no | Expensive*

### GJESTEHUSET LOVISENBERG (U E1) *(ᶆ e1)*

This guesthouse, built in 1878, is not right in the city centre but in the charming suburb of St Hanshaugen. It has been modernised but still takes its guests back to another age with its carefully restored furnishings and lamps and somewhat old-fashioned decor. There is only a television in the lounge. *32 rooms | Lovisenberggata 15a | tel. 22 35 83 00 | www.lovisenberg.no/gjestehuset | Budget*

**INSIDER TIP** ▶ **P-HOTELS OSLO**
**(U E4)** *(ɯ e4)*

A new hotel concept in Norway: 24-hour reception, simple, clean and centrally located. Breakfast (sandwich, juice and fruit) is delivered to your door in the morning. Online booking recommended. *93 rooms | Grensen 19 | tel. 23 31 80 00 | www.photels.no | Moderate*

## INFORMATION

*Oslo Tourist Information* **(U F5)** *(ɯ f5) (Østbanehallen at the main railway station | www.visitoslo.com)*

## WHERE TO GO

### HEDDAL STAVKIRKE ★
**(137 D4)** *(ɯ C17)*

Norway's largest stave church is located right on the E34 near Notodden. It was built around 1200, has three naves and is noteable for its overlapping roofs and intricately carved porch with animal ornaments. The interior is richly decorated, including fine rose paintings. *June–Sept Mon–Sat 10am–5pm, Sun after service from 12:15pm | admission 80 NOK | www.heddalstavkirke.no | 116 km/72 miles southwest of Oslo*

### KONGSBERG **(137 D4)** *(ɯ C16)*

The mining town (pop. 26,500) was founded in 1624 after silver was discovered there. In 1770, almost 10,000 people lived in the town; 4,000 of them worked in the silver mines including many miners

from other parts of Europe. ● A trip on the 2.3 km-long (1½ mile) pit railway of the *Norwegian Mining Museum (mid-May–late Aug daily 10am, noon and 2pm, also at 4pm in July | 160 NOK)*, followed by a one-hour tour of the mine tunnels, is a unique experience. *82 km/51 miles southwest of Oslo*

### TJØME **(137 E5)** *(ɯ D–E17)*

This narrow island that juts into the Skagerrak on the western side of Oslofjord is joined to the mainland by a bridge and is a popular destination for sun worshippers and gourmets. The famous guesthouse *Engø Gård (Gamlke Engø vei 25 | tel. 33 39 00 48 | www.engo.no | Expensive)* is located in a magnificent natural park. Those who prefer just to explore the island may well find themselves at ⚡ *Verdens Ende* – the end of the world. The southern tip is easy to spot thanks to the historic lighthouse from 1932. Its mighty rock is the perfect place for couples to go for a walk on a summer's evening. *On the E18 to Tønsberg and then further to the south on Road 308 | 130 km/80 miles from Oslo*

# TELEMARK

**(136–137 C–D4)** *(ɯ B–C 16–17)* **This region is considered the birthplace of skiing. And the forests are an endless paradise for hikers in summer. In addition, the big lakes and extensive canals make a great variety of holiday experiences possible.**

You can explore the Telemark region at leisure on board the two old ● steamers *Victoria* and *Henrik Ibsen (Fare Skien–Dalen approx. 995 NOK, return half-price, bike 200 NOK | tel. 35 90 00 20 | www.telemarkskanalen.no)* that depart from *Skien* **(137 D5)** *(ɯ C17)* on the south coast in the morning and drop anchor in *Dalen* in the heart of the Telemark in the early evening. If you have a bicycle, the return journey along the banks of the Telemark Canal is a perfect finish to a holiday: You should plan two days for the 120 km/75 mile journey.

## SIGHTSEEING

### RJUKAN

This village (pop. 3,300), which experienced a tremendous industrial boom at the turn of the 20th century, lies wedged between two massive mountain ranges. The day-long hike to ✂ *Gaustatoppen* (1,883 m/6,178 ft) table mountain is rewarded with a panoramic view over much of southern Norway. Rjukan became famous in 2013 when three huge sun mirrors were installed high above the town. Until their arrival, the town was overshadowed by the mountains from October to March. Now sunlight strikes the market square is winter, too. *www.visitrjukan.com*

## WHERE TO STAY

Several spacious cabins to rent on the lake in the village of *Vrådal* (136 C5) *(ጠ C17)*; e.g. *Nisser Hyttesenter (5,000 NOK per week | accommodates up to 8 | tel. 35 05 61 23 | www.hyttesenter.no)*.

### BOKHOTELLET LYNGØRPORTEN ✂

A sea view from every angle. There is no time to waste relaxing and enjoying it though: The hotel keeps you busy offering numerous activities such as fishing, diving or boating to explore the great outdoors. Every room is – as the hotel's name suggests – dedicated to a different genre of literature. *43 rooms | Sliperiveien 18 | Gjeving | tel. 37 19 80 00 | www.bokho tellet.no | Moderate–Expensive*

## INFORMATION

*Skien Turistkontor (Henrik Ibsensgate 2 | Tel. 35 90 55 20 | www.visittelemark.no)*

A tour through the Telemark on a steamboat makes for a leisurely day trip

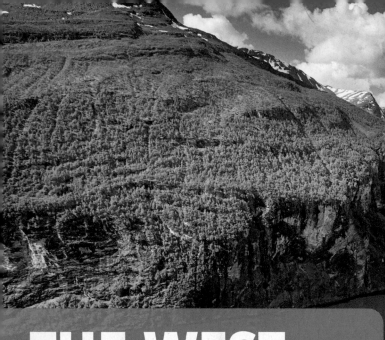

# THE WEST

**Western Norway's frayed coastline is broken up by massive glacial inlets that extend right up to the rock faces of high mountains, forcing those coming over-land to make lengthy detours.**

But such detours can be fascinating be-cause each one takes you to a different landscape and there are new surprises around every bend. The dramatic coun-tryside of western Norway is perfect for relaxing as well as adventures. Winter sports fans and hikers, water sports en-thusiasts and anglers can all find the spot they are looking for between the glaciers and open sea, as can those who just want to discover the gems of Norway's cultural history in the great outdoors in the midst of a fascinating landscape.

# ÅLESUND

**(138 A5)** *(ᗰ B13)* **The port city (pop. 46,000) is surrounded by numer-ous islands and is the most important town – and a major centre of fishing – in the Sunnmøre fjord region.**

After the great fire in 1904 when – in a single day – 850 houses were razed to the ground and 10,000 people left homeless, the new town was recon-structed in the then modern Art Nouveau style. This was supported in part by the German Emperor Wilhelm II. In order to prevent any other conflagrations, stone was used instead of wood for building, lending the town a unique look. The magnificent houses with their towers,

Photo: Geirangerfjord

Fjell, fjords and the coast: western Norway is fjord country – and still the firm favourite for Norway fans

curved gables and decorative elements are located around the picturesque harbour whose canal-like branches divide the town centre.

## SIGHTSEEING

### AKSLA ☼

The hill above Ålesund is not to be missed. You can either climb up the 418 steps to the top or follow the signs to *Fjellstua* in your car. The view sweeps over the town and its harbour, the neighbouring islands, sounds and the sea. And, to the south, the snow-capped peaks of the Sunnmøre Alps come into view – sheer magic!

### JUGENDSTILSENTERET

An exhibition in the former Swan Chemists gives an impression of the architectural style that characterises Ålesund. The authentic furnishings make visitors feel they are back at the beginning of the 20th century. *June–Aug daily 10am–5pm | admission 80 NOK | Apotekergata 16 | www. jugenstilsenteret.no*

A bite to eat at the harbour: The water is always in close reach in Ålesund

### SUNNMØRE MUSEUM

55 old houses and 30 old boats, including Viking ships and a copy of a trading ship from the 11th century, can be seen in this open-air museum. *May–Oct Mon–Fri (also Saturdays in July) 10am–4pm, Sun noon–4pm, otherwise shorter opening hours | admission 80 NOK | Museumsveien 1 | www.sunnmore.museum.no | around 10 km/6¼ miles east of Ålesund*

## FOOD & DRINK

### ANNO

A few surprises are hidden inside the menu of this Italian pizza place, including a pizza with dried cod which you probably can't get anywhere else. The focaccia with seafood delicacies is a treat for your taste buds and just the right thing in this maritime setting. *Apotekergata 9 | tel. 71 70 70 77 | www.anno.no | Moderate*

## SHOPPING

### DEVOLDFABRIKKEN ● ⚓

The factory on the other side of the fjord not only sells the Devold pullovers that are so popular with seafarers, it has extended its range to include sports and leisure clothing made by other manufacturers. Plus there's a café and a magnificent view of the islands off Ålesund. *Mon–Fri 10am–8pm, Sat until 6pm, July/Aug also Sun noon–5pm | ferry to Langevåg from the quay at the central bus station (return Mon–Fri 78 NOK, Sun 50 NOK) | www.devoldfabrikken.no*

## SPORTS & ACTIVITIES

### KAYAK TOURS

The Storfjord, the "Great Fjord", stretches inland from Ålesund – this is the perfect route for day-long excursions into the fjord world. If you didn't bring your kayak with you and would like to join a group, outdoor trips are organ-

ised by *Actin (tel. 92 09 57 45 | www.
actin.no)*.

## WHERE TO STAY

### BORG BED & BREAKFAST

This B & B – a boarding school at other
times of the year – lies 17 km/10½ miles
to the east of Ålesund in beautiful surroundings on the way up the fjord. In the
midst of a forest, you can see the peaks
of the Sunnmøre Alps from the top of the
next hill. The simple rooms are cosy and
they all have their own bathroom; ten
share a kitchen. *June–July | 45 rooms |
Løypevegen 3 | tel. 70 17 76 00 | www.
borgfhs.no/bbb | Budget*

### HOTEL BROSUNDET

After extensive renovations, this designer
hotel, located in a former boathouse, is
one of the most popular places to stay in
the city. The rooms are furnished with an
emphasis on both style and contemporary
comfort. *167 rooms | Apotekergata 1–5 |
tel. 70 10 33 00 | www.brosundet.no |
Expensive*

## INFORMATION

*Destinasjon Ålesund & Sunnmøre (Skate-
flukaia | tel. 70 16 34 30 | www.visit
alesund-geiranger.com*

## WHERE TO GO

### GEIRANGERFJORD ★
(138 B6) *(ꢀ B14)*

The most famous destination and photo motive in western Norway:
Geirangerfjord forces its way inland,
surrounded by steep walls of rock, magnificent waterfalls and mountain mas-
sifs with hidden alpine farms.

You can reach the village of *Geiranger*
by water from ᗺ *Hellesylt*
(80 km/50 miles south-east of Ålesund
on Road 60) with the *car ferry (8 depar-
tures daily | fare 260 NOK per person, car
and driver 530 NOK)* or via winding
roads.

If you take *Road 63* from the south, the
view from ᗺ *Dalsnibba* (1,450 m/
4,750 ft) (toll) will give you the first
impression of what awaits visitors to

---

★ **Geirangerfjord**
Storybook western Norway → **p. 51**

★ **Runde**
Breeding colony for hundreds of
thousands of birds → **p. 52**

★ **Bryggen**
Stroll between the old wooden
houses in the old Hanseatic city of
Bergen → **p. 53**

★ **Hardangervidda**
The most extensive plateau area in
Europe and the ultimate hiking expe-
rience at any time of the year → **p. 58**

★ **Vøringfossen**
Roaring waterfall in the heart of
western Norway → **p. 58**

★ **Borgund Stavkirke**
The jewel among Norway's stave
churches → **p. 60**

★ **Flåms railway**
A trip through steep mountain
scenery → **p. 61**

★ **Preikestolen**
Tiny rocky plateau soaring above the
Lysefjord below – an uplifting sight
→ **p. 63**

**MARCO POLO HIGHLIGHTS**

Geirangerfjord. From Åndalsnes (138 B5) (*ↄↄↄ B13*), the ⊿ *Trollstigveien* hair-pin bends and the lookout points of ⊿ *Ørnesvingen* offer magnificent vistas of the Sunnmøre mountains. The most beautiful alternative route in this part of Norway leads to an idyllic valley and **INSIDER TIP** *Petrines Gyestgiveri (10 rooms, 5 flats | Norddal | Riksvei 63 | tel. 92 23 48 20 | www.petrines.com | Budget)* – a guesthouse where you will feel at home and where blissful meals are served using the freshest of produce available (don't forget to try the strawberries). *www.geiranger.no*

## GODØY
### (138 A5) (*ↄↄↄ B13*)

Two underwater tunnels and a bridge lead to this small island off the coast of Ålesund. On the way, you can visit the island of *Giske* with its beautifully-located marble church from the 11th century. The ⊿ **INSIDER TIP** *Alnys fyr* lighthouse *(June–Aug daily, otherwise only Sun 11am–6pm | tours 25 NOK)* that was erected on Godøy in 1936 is an important landmark. A café serves delicious home-made cakes and snacks.

## RUNDE ★
### (138 A5) (*ↄↄↄ A13*)

The west of the island in the Ålesund shipping channel is a densely populated bird rock whose most important attraction are the hundreds of thousands of puffins that spend the summer here. The hike up to the ⊿ cliffs takes about one hour and you will not only be rewarded by the birds but also the magnificent view over the Norwegian Sea and the bracing ocean wind. Boat trips to the bird island depart from Ålesund. *75 km/47 miles west of Ålesund | ferry from Sulasundet to Hareid (36 departures daily)*

# BERGEN

(136 A3) (*ↄↄↄ A15*) **Yes, it's true: Bergen has one of the highest rainfalls of any city on earth. But, when the sun does break through the clouds, all seats in the pavement cafés and restaurants are taken in a jiffy – no matter which direction the wind is blowing from or how cold it is.**

Bergen was founded in 1070 and today has a population of 273,000 making it Norway's second-largest city. It has a glorious past as a royal seat, a port and a member of the Hanseatic League.

Bergen was the largest city in northern Europe in the Middle Ages. The Bryggen harbour quarter was in the hands of the Hansa from the 14th century and the last northern German merchants did not leave until 1764.

The *Bergen Card (24 hours 240 NOK, 48 hours 310 NOK | available from the tourist information office, railway station and other places)* offers a 30 per cent discount on the largest multi-storey car park, Bygarasjen, as well as free, or substantially reduced, entrance fees to most of the sights in the city. If you plan to stay overnight in summer, you should book your accommodation well in advance.

## SIGHTSEEING

### AKVARIET ●

You will not only be able to see local marine animals in western Norway's largest aquarium – crocodiles, exotic ocean dwellers and snakes are also on display. Families with children will be delighted by the seals and penguins, and there is also a pool where you can put your hands in the water and really come into contact with the fish and crustaceans. *May–Aug daily 10am–6pm, otherwise 10am–4pm | admission 270 NOK | www.akvariet.no*

Splendid sight with or without your umbrella: the old merchant houses in Bryggen

### BERGENSHUS FESTNING ☀

The *Håkonshalle*, built in 1261 in the Gothic style, is the heart of the Bergenshus fortress complex (a landmark for sailors visible from afar) and is used today for concerts and other festive events. Construction of the neighbouring, massive *Rosary Tower* as a residence and defence installation was completed in 1568. *In summer daily 10am–4pm, otherwise shorter opening hours | admission 80 NOK | www.bymuseet.no*

### BRYGGEN ★

What is possibly the most famous district in Norway was in the hands of merchants from Lübeck for more than 400 years. Today, it is a Unesco World Heritage Site and just as lively as ever. A stroll through the old Hanseatic quarter, which was reconstructed after a major fire in 1702, could begin in the historic Finnegården courtyard of the *Hanseatic Museum (June–Aug daily 9am–5pm, otherwise shorter opening times | admission 160* NOK | *www.museumvest.no) and end in Bryggens Museum (May–Aug daily 10am–4pm, otherwise shorter opening hours | admission 80 NOK | www.bymuseet.no).* Between these two, you will be able to take a look at the last preserved – albeit reconstructed – *Shøtstue (included in the entrance fee for the Hanseatic Museum)* where the Hanseatic merchants held their meetings according to strict rules and enjoyed an evening drinking.

### FISKETORGET (FISH MARKET)

The fresh fish, fruits, vegetables and flowers are of premium quality, but the prices are somewhat higher than elsewhere. If you have the misfortune of being in Bergen on a rainy day, take shelter in the glass *Mathallen* on the southern shore that also has some restaurants. *June–Aug daily 7am–8pm, otherwise Mon–Sat 9am–5pm*

### FLØYEN ☀

This lookout hill has a firm place in the hearts of the people of Bergen; it rises up

All of Bergen at your feet – panoramic view from the Fløyen lookout hill

319 m (1,050 ft) above the town centre and provides a magnificent view over the city and surrounding islands as far as the open sea. You can reach the summit in eight minutes with the *Fløiban (Mon–Fri 7:30am–11pm, Sat/Sun 8am–11pm | one-way fare 45 NOK | www.floibanen.no)*.

## KODE

This acronym stands for the four collections of Bergen's art museum, which are situated almost right next to each other. *Kode 1 (Nordahl Bruns gate 1)* is dedicated to handicrafts and design; one of its special exhibits is the *Sölvskatten,* a collection of some 600 gold and silver items crafted in Bergen. *Kode 2 (Rasmus Meyer allé 6)* houses excellent temporary exhibits of an international calibre plus the café *Smakverket* on the ground floor which is the perfect place for a snack. The famous Rasmus Meyer Collection featuring Norwegian works of art by artists such as Edvard Munch, Christian Krogh, J. C. Dahl, Harriet Backer and others graces the walls

of *Kode 3 (Rasmus Meyer allé 7)*. It also has a noteworthy collection of sketches and graphics by Edvard Munch. The permanent exhibit in *Kode 4 (Lysverket)* takes you on a journey through art history from the Renaissance to the 20th century. The *KunstLab* on the ground floor is dedicated to children. *Mid-May–Aug daily 11am–5pm, otherwise Tue–Sun 11am–4pm | admission 100 NOK | www.kodebergen.no*

### INSIDER TIP LEPRAMUSEET

A strange subject for a museum maybe but a visit will give a different perspective on this disease. Housed in the former Sankt Jørgens Hospital where Dr Armauer Hansen discovered the disease in 1873, the museum exhibits photos and historic documents recording the lives of leper patients and their fates. Be warned: some of the photos are rather gruesome to look at. *In summer daily 11am–3pm | admission 70 NOK | St-Jørgens-Hospital | Kong Oscars gate 59 | www.bymuseet.no*

## ULRIKEN

On the cable car ride to the highest peak in Bergen, the view of the city and its surrounding area expands as far as the eye can see with every metre that you climb. Bergen's mountain basin location, the countless offshore islands and even ships on the horizon come into view if the weather conditions are favourable. Once you've reached the top, you should take the time for a hike through the Alpine landscape on Ulriken's ridge. *Cable car May–Sept 9am–9pm, otherwise only until 5pm | return trip 170 NOK; 2-hour panoramic tour from the city centre 270 NOK | bus 2, 4, 9 Haukeland sykehus*

## FOOD & DRINK

### CAFÉ OPERA

This small café-restaurant has been popular for almost three decades. The reasons for its success lie in its location between the university and city centre as well as the short menu with excellent dishes and the dedication to providing a stage for music and art. *Engen 18 | www.cafeopera.org | Budget*

### ENHJØRNINGEN/TO KOKKER

Bergen's best fish dishes are served in *Enhjørningen* in the Hanseatic Enhjørningsgården courtyard in Bryggen. *To kokker* in the same house specialises in meat dishes. *Enhjørningen tel. 55 30 69 50 | To kokker tel. 55 30 69 55 | www.enhjørningen.no | Expensive*

**INSIDER TIP** ▶ MARG & BEIN ☺

Not far from the university, the award-winning chef Hanne Frosta offers fans of refined cuisine just what they are looking for. How about pollack and seaweed or herring and trout roe? All the ingredients are sourced from the region or fresh from the sea. *Fosswinckelsgate 18 | tel. 55 32 34 32 | www.marg-bein.no | Moderate*

## SHOPPING

*Galleriet (Torgallmenning)* in the centre of town has a total of almost 60 shops under a single roof. You will be able to buy arts and crafts in the small shops on *Lille Øvregate* to the right of the Fløibanen; the Bergen branch of *Husfliden (www.norskflid.no/bergen)* is located directly behind the Tourist Information Office. On *Strandkaien* opposite Bryggen, you will find the shop of the exclusive Norwegian woollen fashion brand *Oleana (www.oleana.no)* and 100 metres further on *Strandkalen Fisk* is the right place to go for warm *fiskekaker*. On about 20 Saturdays a year, a farmer's market is held in front of the granaries in

## LOW BUDGET

The best and possibly cheapest pizza (from 110 NOK) in Bergen can be had at *Pasta Sentral (Vestre Torggate 5–7 | tel. 55 99 00 37 | www.pastasentral.no)*

The *Hardanger Hostel* has a dreamlike location high above Hardangerfjord *(season July–15 Aug | double room 950 NOK | tel. 53 67 14 00 | www.hardangerhostel.no)*

The simply furnished rooms in *Marken Gjestehus (22 rooms | Kong Oscars gate 45 | tel. 55 31 44 04 | www.marken-gjestehus.com)* in Bergen are painted in welcoming colours and the atmosphere is friendly. If you sleep in a four-bed room, you will pay 290 NOK a night.

Bryggen called the ⚲ *Bondens marked* *(www.bondensmarked.no)*. Almost all the stalls feature exclusively organic products from the region, ranging from honey to mutton and cheese to cake.

## ENTERTAINMENT

It is easy to tell that Bergen is a town with lots of students and an innovative international music scene if you go to concerts at the *Garage (Christies gate 14 | www. garage.no)*, *Det Akademiske Kvarteret (Olv Kyrres gate 49 | www.kvarteret.no)* and *USF (Georgernes verft 12 | www.usf. no)*.

On warm summer evenings, take a stroll around the city soaking in its beguiling vibes. Start your evening at the *Kippers* coffee shop in the USF. With a bit of luck, the other guests will tell you where's the coolest place to head next.

### HENRIK ØL & VINSTUE
This is the perfect place to start your evening in Bergen. An extensive selection of British, German and Norwegian beers, not too much noise and nice people in front of – and behind – the bar. *Engen 10*

### PINGVINEN
Absolutely trendy – because of the relaxed atmosphere, the extensive list of beers and the traditional Norwegian food *(Budget)*. *Vaskerelven 14 | tel. 55 60 46 46*

## WHERE TO STAY

### AUGUSTIN HOTEL ☘
This stylish and cosy family-run hotel is sits directly on the harbour bay of Vågen. Guests can enjoy a fantastic view of the harbour and the historic Bryggen quarter on the other side of the shore from many of the rooms. *130 rooms | C.*

*Sundts gate 22 | tel. 55 30 40 00 | www. augustin.no | Expensive*

### KLOSTERHAGEN HOTELL ☘
A ten minute's walk from the Fish Market and surrounded by wonderfully restored wooden houses, this hotel offers the best view of the city and the mountains plus top-notch comfort and service. It is truly a place to unwind. *15 rooms | Strangehagen 2 | tel. 53 00 22 00 | www.kloster hagenhotell.no | Moderate*

### SKANSEN PENSJONAT
Just a few steps above the Fløibahn, right in the middle of the town, this small inn makes for a friendly home away from home. *7 rooms, 1 flat | Vetrlidsallmenningen 29 | tel. 55 31 90 80 | www. skansen-pensjonat.no | Moderate*

## INFORMATION

*Turistinformasjon (Strandkaien 3 | tel. 55 55 20 00 | www.visitbergen.com)*

## WHERE TO GO

### LYSØEN (136 A3) (ᗕ A16)
Its rustic mix of styles makes the country home of Bergen's miraculous violinist Ole Bull (1810–88) on a small island in Fanafjord well worth seeing. The visit comes along with a short boat trip. *Daily in summer, otherwise only Sun 11am–4pm | admission 60 NOK incl. guided tour, boat transfer 60 NOK | www.lysoen.no | 25 km/15½ miles south of Bergen on Road 553*

### TROLDHAUGEN/GRIEG MUSEUM AND HOME (136 A3) (ᗕ A15)
For 22 years, this villa on a promontory in Nordåsvannet Lake was the home of Edvard Grieg and his wife Nina between spring and autumn. The small cabin near

the water that Grieg used for composing inspired him to many world-famous works. Concerts are held regularly in summer in the well-hidden *Troldsalen* such as the INSIDERTIP 30-minute lunch concerts with a tour of the house and museum afterwards *(daily | 160 NOK). May–Sept daily 9am–6pm | admission 100 NOK | Troldhaugveien 65 | www.grieg-museum.no | 10 km/6¼ miles south of Bergen | take the Bybanen tram to the stop "Hop").*

Especially when the snow melts, these wet wonders that are the "gate to Hardanger" spray their fine mist over all the cars and observers. Hundreds of thousands of fruit trees grow between the forested slopes and the *Hardangerfjord* that shimmers a bluish-green in summer. The blossoming fruit trees at the end of April – when people are still skiing just a few hundred metres further up the slope – are an absolute highlight.

# HARDANGER

*(136 B–C 3–4) (□ B15–16)* **The Folgefonna Glacier towers over the region Hardanger to the side of the Hardangerfjord that extends inland to the south of Bergen as far as the high Hardangervidda plateau.**
Waterfalls in every direction: the *Steinsdalsfossen* in the west, the *Tveitefossen* in the north, the *Vøringfossen* in the east and the *Låtefossen* in the south.

## SIGHTSEEING

### HARDANGER-FARTØYVERNSENTERET (HARDANGER MUSEUM SHIPYARD)
Ever fancied building a real boat? Then try your luck here. Professionals will first show you how they repair old sailing boats and schooners and then it's your turn to swing the hammer. The shipyard exudes authentic charm with its smells of seawater, wood and tar. Guided tours in summer, café. *May–Aug daily 10am–5pm | admission 90 NOK | Norhelmsund | www.hardangerogvossmuseum.no*

Mountain peaks and glaciers within one's reach on the Hardangerfjord

### HARDANGERVIDDA ★

This is the largest high-altitude plateau in Europe, extending over an area of 9,000 km² (3,475 miles²), and is the Norwegian hiking area *per se*. The well-marked paths that criss-cross the barren, 1,000 to 1,600 m (3,200–5,200 ft)-high plateau only come to light between June and September. The flora is limited to stunted birch trees, grass and lichen but the fauna has many surprises in store: birds of prey, lemmings and Europe's most southerly reindeer herds.

The only real peaks are in the west; hiking is completely safe and nights can be spent in self-catering cabins or professionally run accommodation, or even in your own tent. The best places to start your hike on the "Vidda" are Road 7 on the northern border and the E 134 on the south-eastern periphery near *Røldal*. A strenuous but beautiful climb ends at ⬇ *Munkentrappene* near *Lofthus* (Road 13) on the western border of the Hardangervidda, the route having been constructed by monks in the 13th century. An even more dramatic climb is from Kinsarvik through *Husedalen*, the "Valley of the Waterfalls".

### HARDANGERVIDDA NATURCENTER

Those who don't want to discover Hardangervidda only on a hike can get a detailed overview of the natural and cultural history of the plateau at this centre. The kitchen staff in the *restaurant (tel. 53 66 59 00 | Budget)* conjure up excellent traditional meals. *April–Oct daily 10am–6pm, 15 June–20 Aug 9am–7pm | admission 130 NOK | Øvre Eidfjord | www.hardangerviddanatursenter.no*

Free fall: the Vøringfossen

### VØRINGFOSSEN ★ ⬇

You will hardly be able to see all the way down to the bottom of this easily accessible waterfall but the view over the thundering water and deep gorge is all the more exciting. Please be careful and mind the guardrails! Every second, 12 m³ (424 ft³) of water plummets into the ravine. The gigantic ⬇ *Sysendamm* is located just a few miles away towards the Hardangervidda. There you will have a wonderful view of the valley and Hardangerjøkulen Glacier.

### FOOD & DRINK

#### STEINSTØ FRUKTGARD ⬇

This café serves fruit and berries from Hardanger, Norwegian home-style cooking – and a breathtaking view over the fjord and fjell. *Fykesundvegen 768 |*

*Steinstø | on Road 7 | tel. 99 69 15 27 | www. steinsto-fruktgard.no | Budget*

### INSIDER TIP VILTKROA

Organic gourmet meals at the camping site *Måbødalen Camping (Øvre Eidfjord | tel. 53 66 59 88 | www.mabodalen.no | Moderate)*: trout, reindeer and lots of veggies.

## WHERE TO STAY

### HARDANGER GJESTEGARD

A former fruit press forms the core of this orchard guesthouse where the machines and wine cellar have been preserved. *7 rooms | Alsåker | Utne | tel. 97 10 18 78 | www.hardanger-gjestegard.no | Moderate*

## INFORMATION

*Reisemål Hardangerfjord (Norheimsund | tel. 56 55 38 70 | www.hardangerfjord.com)*

# MOLDE

**(138 B5)** *(∅ B13)* **This quiet backwater (pop. 26,500) is turned on its head every year when international jazz musicians arrive here to jam at its annual festival.**

The surrounding countryside has a lot to offer with its exciting juxtaposition of mountains, fjords and the open sea. There is a splendid view of the Romsdalen peaks from the more modest ☆ Varden Mountain (407 m, 1,350 ft) on the northern outskirts of the town.

## SIGHTSEEING

### KRONA ROMSDALSMUSEET

Opened in 2016, the new museum building seems to stand like a lofty ship's mast in its surroundings. For art lovers, there is a permanent exhibition dedicated to the German painter Kurt Schwitters, who lived on the island of Hjertøya from 1932–39. *June–Aug daily 11am–5pm, otherwise shorter opening times | admission 100 NOK | Per Amdams veg 4 | www.roms dalsmuseet.no*

## FOOD & DRINK

### FOLE GODT

Urban coffee house culture on a latitude of 62 degrees: This cosy, authentic café welcomes you to take a wellearned break. Everything is home baked and made with love. The sandwiches are extremely delicious – try the one filled with roast beef and rémoulade made according to their own recipe *Storgata 61*

## SPORTS & ACTIVITIES

### INSIDER TIP CYCLING BY THE SEA

Discover the islands off the coast of Molde by bike. You will hardly ever be bothered by cars as you make your way from one island to the next; there will be the taste of salt on your lips and a peaceful bay around the next bend. The tour over three islands, starting in Molde, is 200 km/125 miles long.

## WHERE TO STAY

### HUSTADVIKA GJESTEGÅRD

This guesthouse, built on the ruins of a fish trading post, is located in Farstad, about 50 km/31 miles to the north of Molde. *17 rooms, 14 cabins | Storholmen | tel. 71 26 47 00 | www.hustadvika.no | Moderate*

### SCANDIC SEILET ☆

In Molde, directly on the fjord, shaped like an giant sail. Most rooms have magical views. Spa and landscaped swimming

small islands and skerries with each other to the island of *Averøya* and further to the port of *Kristiansund (www.visitkristiansund.com)*. There are places to stop and even go fishing on both sides of the road.

# SOGNEFJORD

**(136 A–C2)** *(⌂ A–B14–15)* **A gigantic estuary and towering mountains on both sides characterize Norway's longest and deepest fjord.**

Even today, travellers have to rely on the ferries that cross the fjord at all times of the day. Some of the side arms of the *Sognefjord* are famous tourist attractions created by Mother Nature. The Aurlandsfjord and Nærøyfjord – one of the narrowest navigable fjords – are Unesco World Heritage Sites.

The art of building with wood,
12th century: Borgund Stavkirke

area. *224 rooms | tel. 71 11 40 00 | www.scandichotels.com | Moderate*

## INFORMATION

*Turistinformasjon (Torget 4 | tel. 70 23 88 00 | www.visitmolde.com)*

## WHERE TO GO

### ATLANTIC OCEAN ROUTE ● ⚹
**(138 B4–5)** *(⌂ B12–13 )*

This route starts in the idyllic fishing village of *Bud* and proceeds northwards along the Hustadvika section of the coast that was feared by seafarers on account of its unpredictable winds and currents – and, you can be assured that you will still have close contact with the elements! You travel over eight bridges that connect

## SIGHTSEEING

### BALESTRAND ⚹

The countryside and the light have attracted artists to this small village at the widest point of Sognefjord for 150 years. Peace and quiet reign between the pretty houses – including some galleries – and the view over the fjord is unsurpassed. You can spend the night in *Kviknes Hotel (190 rooms | tel. 57 69 42 00 | www.kviknes.no | Expensive)* a fairy-tale hotel in the Swiss style whose reception rooms also function as a museum. The **INSIDER TIP** *ferry from Balestrand to Fjærland (June–Aug daily 8am and noon)* steers northwards through *Fjærlandfjord* directly towards an arm of *Jostedalsbreen*, the largest glacier in continental Europe.

### BORGUND STAVKIRKE ★ ●

The most famous of Norway's stave churches (built around 1180) is on the E16 30 km/19 miles to the east of Lærdal, a small town at the eastern end of

Sognefjord. The dragon heads on the gable and wonderful carvings on the west entrance are especially striking. If there are too many tourists, it can be worth changing your plans and visiting the stave church in *Undredal. May–Sept daily 10am–5pm (mid-June–mid-Aug 8am–8pm) | admission 90 NOK | www.stavkirke.no*

## FLÅMSBANA ★

Past gushing waterfalls, deep ravines and through narrow tunnels – without exaggeration, this is the world's most spectacular train ride. The train runs from *Myrdal* at a height of 866 m/2,906 ft down the mountain to the small town of *Flåm,* the journey taking approximately one hour. If you prefer to stretch your feet and soak in the spectacular scenery, take the train up the mountain to Myrdal instead and then ride back into the valley by bike. *Fares from 420 NOK | tours from Bergen | www.visitflam.com*

## NORSK BREMUSEUM

This architecturally interesting museum focuses on Jostedalsbreen Glacier and includes exhibitions, models and a wide-screen film. It is located in Fjærland at the foot of the Bøyabreen and Suphellebreen glacier arms. *April–May and Sept–Oct 10am–4pm, June–Aug 9am–7pm | admission 125 NOK | www.bre.museum.no*

## STEGASTEINEN ● ☼

While paragliders use the platform as a jumping point, everyone else stands in front of the glass rail to admire the spectacular fjord view (if good weather prevails) and the long drop below. You have two options to return to safe ground – jump by paraglide or simply walk down the 30 m/98 ft – what will you choose? *On the Aurlandsvegen pass road between Aurland and Lærdal, turn off shortly after Aurland*

## UNDREDAL STAVKIRKE

The smallest church in Scandinavia lies hidden between the gigantic mountain scenery on the shore of Aurlandfjord 13 km/8 miles to the north of Flåm. The church is only 4 m/13 ft wide and was probably built in the 12th century. The village of Undredal is also famous for its goat's cheese.

## INFORMATION

In summer, you can find tourist information offices on both sides of the Sognefjord in several towns. *Tel. 99 23 15 00 | www.sognefjord.no*

## WHERE TO GO

### NORDFJORD (136 B1) (𝄜 B14)

Pretty villages and high hills that invite tourists to take long hikes lie on both sides of Nordfjord beneath the gigantic Jostedalsbreen glacier. Trips to the Briksdalsbreen glacier snout *(mid-April–mid-Oct daily 8:15am–5pm | bookings tel. 57 87 68 05 | 205 NOK | www.oldedalen-skysslag.com)* start in *Oldedalen* 22 km/14 miles after the signposted turnoff in *Olden* (185 km/116 miles north of Balestrand). A more economical alternative is to travel along the Loenvatnet Lake from *Loen* to the valley end of *Kjenndal.* From there, it is only a fifteen-minute walk to the Kjenndalsbreen glacial arm. *Further Information: Reisemål Stryn & Nordfjord (tel. 57 87 40 40 | www.nordfjord.no)*

### VESTKAPP (136 A–B1) (𝄜 A–B13–14)

Ships depart for the ruins of the *Selje Monastery (mid-June–mid-August daily 10am and 1:15 pm | 275 NOK | tickets from the Tourist Information Office | tel. 40 44 60 11 | www.seljekloster.no)* from the harbour at *Selje* (245 km/155 miles from Balestrand). The monastery was erected by Benedictine monks at the beginning of the 12th century in honour of St Sunniva, the patron saint of western Norway. You will discover a wonderful sand beach in *Ervik* below Vestkapp. *Vestkapp Camping (cabins for 4 or 6 | tel. 57 85 99 50 | www. vestkappcamping.com | Budget)* at the turn off to the village is the perfect starting point for a trip to ☼ Vestkapp that is a mere 3 km (1.8 mile) away. The almost 500-m-high (1,640 ft) rock *Kjerringa* towers over the Stadlandet coast that is feared for its changing winds and currents.

# STAVANGER

**(136 B5) (∅ A17) From a sleepy fishing village to a booming oil capital – Stavanger (pop. 131,000) shows how it is done.**
Life in the streets in the old town *(Gamle Stavanger)* to the west of Vågen harbour bay is quite peaceful amongst the white wooden houses while the shore on the other side is lined with shops, bars and restaurants.

## SIGHTSEEING

### NORSK HERMETIKKMUSEUM
What can be interesting about a museum for tinned food? Well, there are some things, especially when in this former canning factory you feel like it's 1920 and any minute you'll meet workers canning sardines and sending them out into the world. *Mid-May–Sept daily 10am–4pm | admission 90 NOK | Øvre Strandgate 88 | www.museumstavanger.no*

### NORSK OLJEMUSEUM
The interactive oil museum shows how black gold evolves and is used, and how the offshore adventure has transformed Norway. *June–Aug daily 10am–7pm, Sept–* *May Mon–Sat 10am–4pm, Sun 10am–6pm | admission 120 NOK | Kjeringholmen 1 | www.norskolje.museum.no*

## FOOD & DRINK

### BEVAREMEGVEL
The name is a figure of speech – something along the lines of "you must be joking!" Varied lunch menu, daily specials until 6pm. *Skagen 12 | tel. 51 84 38 60 | www.herlige-restauranter.no/bevare megvel | Expensive*

## SHOPPING

### INSIDER TIP JANS FISKERØYKERI
Home of Norway's best smoked salmon, produced here in chambers from the post-war years. Gourmets from all over Europe regularly come to stock up on gravlax or smoked salmon. *Johannes gate 37*

## BEACHES

Thanks to the Ice Age and the Gulf Stream, there are wonderful sandy beaches with dunes for sunbathing near Stavanger. The Jæren beaches start to the south. The most delightful are *Borestranda* (around 15 km/9½ miles south of the airport) and *Orrestranda* (22 km/14 miles to the south). The sandy ☼ INSIDER TIP *Sandvestranden,* which is surrounded by cliffs a little to the north of the picturesque harbour town Skudeneshavn on Karmøy (22 km/14 miles north of Stavanger, ferry), offers a magnificent view of the North Sea and plenty of room to stretch your legs even on warm summer days.

## ENTERTAINMENT

It is really lively on the quay and in the small streets on the northern side of Vågen Bay; there is plenty of action until

A feeling of flying: those with a head for heights are treated to spectacular views from the Preikestolen

closing time *(clubs at 3:30am; other venues 2am)*. *Cardinal Pub & Bar (Skagen 21| www.cardinal.no)* has Norway's largest selection of beer with more than 500 varieties.

## WHERE TO STAY

### FIRST HOTEL ALSTOR

A modern building with spacious rooms. The evening buffet is included in the price. Situated on Mosvatnet Lake, 2 km (1.2 mile) from the town centre. *81 rooms | Tjensvollveien 31 | tel. 52 04 40 00 | www. firsthotels.com | Moderate*

### SOLA STRAND HOTEL ●

This peaceful oasis lies to the south, near the airport, and features a spa, swimming pool and sauna. The white building, from 1914, the dunes, sky and sea, all combine to create a harmonious whole. *139 rooms | Axel Lunds veg 27 | tel. 51 94 30 00 | www.sola-strandhotel.no | Expensive*

## INFORMATION

*Turistinformasjon (Domkirkeplassen 3 | tel. 51 85 92 00 | www.regionstavanger.com)*

## WHERE TO GO

### PREIKESTOLEN ★ ● ☼
### (136 B5) *(ጠ A–B17)*

Now you'd only have to know how to fly and everything would be perfect! If you have been willing to tackle the two-hour hike (one way) to the 604 m/1,980 ft high plateau that only measures 625 m²/6,727 sq ft, you'll be rewarded by the great view over Lysefjord. No railings and no barrier will stop you here – while some still wrestle with their fear of heights, others already sit down and boldly let their feet dangle over the abyss. And now set up the barbecue you brought and have a picnic accompanied by the subline scenery around you!

# TRØNDELAG

**The area around the cathedral and university city of Trondheim offers a variety of stunning scenery.**

The mountains in the south are popular places for skiing and hiking. The Trondheimsfjord with its various arms is bordered by pasture land through which some of the best salmon rivers in the country wind their way. But, above all, Trøndelag is an eldorado for anyone interested in history.

# DOVREFJELL

(138–139 C–D 5–6) (*C13–14*) **The Dovrefjell mountain region with the national park of the same name is the gateway to Trøndelag.**

The E6 makes its way through the mountain range where 2,500 wild reindeer and 130 musk oxen roam. Botanists are attracted by the richness of the plant life that can be found here and geologist are fascinated by the moraines, eskers and other deposits that were formed during the last Ice Age. The most important town in the region, the alpine centre *Oppdal*, is popular with families with children.

## SIGHTSEEING

The *Kongsvold Fjeldstue (www.kongsvold. no)* hotel has a long history as a mountain guesthouse and is, at the same time, also a station for botanic and zoological research. A fantastic place to enjoy the mountains of the Dovrefjell-Sunndalsfjella National

The region around Trondheim: a weather-beaten coastline, a fertile hinterland and the centre of Norway's ecclesiastical history

Park is the ☀ **INSIDER TIP** *Viewpoint Snøhetta* – a prize-winning flat-roofed construction made of glass and steel situated at a height of 1,500 m (4,921 ft). Leaving from Hjerkinn, drive west to the car park Tverrfjellet and then the last 1.5 km (1 mile) is just an easy walk. A visit to Dovrefjell isn't complete without a *musk ox or elk safari (from Kongsvold or Oppdal Turistbüro | mid-June–late Aug | duration approx. 5 hours | costs 425 NOK | www. moskussafari.no). Kongsvold is 43 km/27 miles north of Dombås on the E 6*

## WHERE TO STAY

### SKIFER HOTEL ☀
The glass and slate façade may seem a bit cold, but the 177 rooms offer a delightful view. *O. Skasliens vei 9 | Oppdal | tel. 73 60 50 80 | www.skiferhotel.no | Moderate*

### INSIDER TIP SMEGARDEN CAMPING
Camping site with pretty cabins and well-kept sanitary facilities. Fantastic location on a slope, near the E 6, but still very

peaceful. *Oppdal | tel. 72 42 41 59 | www.smegarden.no | Budget*

## INFORMATION

*Oppdal Turistkontor (O. Skarsliens vei 24 | tel. 72 40 04 70 | www.oppdal.com)*

# RØROS

(139 D5) (*∅ D13*) ★ **Time seems to have come to a standstill in the former copper-mining town (pop. 5,600) near the Swedish border.**

The church – the only stone building as far as the eye can see – towers above the rows of around 50 listed houses on the two main streets.

Røros is a winter-holiday resort: the temperature can sink to minus 30°C (–22°F) but, in this dry inland climate, a sleigh ride is still a great experience.

## SIGHTSEEING

### OLAVSGRUVA (OLAV'S PIT)

This copper mine is located 13 km /8 miles east on Road 31 towards Sweden. *Tours 20 June–15 Aug daily 11am, 1pm, 3pm and 5pm, 16 Aug–10 Sept daily 3pm | admission 120 NOK | www.rorosmuseet.no*

### INSIDER TIP SMELTHYTTA (SMELTERY)

An excellent museum that gives you an idea of how a mine functions. On the outskirts of town next to the gigantic slag heaps. *16 Aug–10 Sept daily 10am–6pm, 11 Sept–May 10am–3pm, 1–19 June 10am–4pm | admission 100 NOK | www.rorosmuseet.no*

## FOOD & DRINK

### INSIDER TIP LOCAL FOOD SAFARI ☺

Five-hour bus trip with reindeer, elk, venison and trout tastings plus a visit to a game slaughterhouse and a farm bak-

Shopping in the old copper town: the centre of Røros

ery as well as lunch in a historic inn. *Daily in summer at 10am | 720 NOK | book in advance before 5:30pm on the day prior at Røros Turistkontor*

## WHERE TO STAY

### VINGELS GAARD GJESTGIVERI
Rustic guesthouse at 750 m /2,500 ft with alpine pastures and a magnificent hiking and mountain biking area. *10 rooms | Gardsjordet | Vingelen | tel. 99 36 82 62 | www.vingelsgaard.no | Moderate*

## INFORMATION

*Røros Turistkontor (Peder Hiortsgata 2 | tel. 72 41 00 00 | www.roros.no)*

# TRONDHEIM

**(139 D4)** *(M D12)* **Originally founded in 997, Trondheim was the capital of Norway from 1030 to 1217, and the seat of the Norwegian archbishops until the Reformation in 1536. Pilgrims also made the trek to the town as they believed that the Saint Olav's tomb was buried beneath the cathedral.**

The *Nidarosdomen* is Norway's only cathedral and the most important sight in this city (pop. 191,000) best known today for its University of Technology and internationally renowned research institutions.

## SIGHTSEEING

### ERKEBISPEGÅRDEN
The archbishop's palace was the political and spiritual centre from the middle of the 12th century but, after the Reformation, became the residence of the northern Norwegian feudal lords and later a military depot. Archaeological finds, religious sculptures and weapons are on display

**CITY WHERE TO START?**
**Nidarosdomen:** The cathedral is both your first destination and starting point. You can reach it by car via the E6. Coming from the south, turn off into the Lade suburb and park at the *City Syd Shopping Centre*, which has regular bus service to the centre. From the north, follow signs to the centre and the *Leuthenhaven multi-storey car park (closed Sunday | Erling Skakkes gate 40)*.

here. *June–Aug Mon–Fri 9am–6pm, Sat 10am–2pm, Sun 1pm–5pm, otherwise shorter opening hours | admission 90 NOK or 180 NOK including the cathedral*

### GAMLE BYBRO (OLD CITY BRIDGE)
This bridge was built in 1861 and leads from the city centre to the *Bakklandet* district with its narrow streets and pretty INSIDER TIP▶ wooden houses. The Trond-

★ **Røros**
A journey back in time to the heyday of copper mining → p. 66

★ **Munkholmen**
Small island facing Trondheim with a "captivating" past → p. 68

★ **Nidarosdomen**
Climb the western tower and be stunned by the view of Trondheim → p. 68

★ **Ringve Museum**
Magnificent building in Trondheim housing the Music Museum → p. 68

MARCO POLO HIGHLIGHTS

Looks back on a millennium:
Nidaros Cathedral in Trondheim

scending into Scandinavia's largest medieval building which has welcomed many a royal guest, the last being Princess Märtha Louise who married Ari Behn here in 2002. *June–Aug Mon–Fri 9am–6pm, Sat 9am–2pm, Sun 1pm–5pm, otherwise shorter opening times | admission 90 NOK | www.nidarosdomen.no*

### RINGVE MUSEUM ★

*Ringve Gård* manor house from the 18th century lies in a magnificent park on the eastern outskirts of the city and is now the site of a music museum. It is even possible to play some of the instruments (at *prøv selv-stasjoner* – try-yourself-stations) in the collection exhibited in a renovated barn. *June–Aug daily 10am–5pm, May daily, Sept–April Tue–Sun 11am–4pm, guided tours 2pm in summer | admission 130 NOK | Lade | www.ringve.no*

### INSIDER TIP ▶ ROCKHEIM

This "time tunnel" documenting the history of Norwegian rock and pop music under the motto "Do you remember" is interesting even if you aren't Norwegian. *Tue–Sun 11am–6pm | admission 130 NOK | Brattøykaia 14 | www.rockheim.no*

### STIFTSGÅRDEN

The 58 m/190 ft long city court was completed in 1778 and the rooms and furnishings are characteristic of the Rococo period. When walking through the halls, visitors have the feeling that they are promenading through a wooden palace. *June–20 Aug Mon–Sat 10am–3pm, Sun noon–3pm (tours every hour) | admission 90 NOK | Munkegata 23*

### VITENSKAPSMUSEUM

The Museum of Science shows archeological finds from the Stone Age to the Viking period. Rewarding exhibitions on medieval Trondheim and religious art to

heimers lovingly call the red superstructure the "Door to Happiness".

### MUNKHOLMEN ★ ⠵

A small island in the fjord facing the city with very well preserved monastic ruins. This is where chiefs were beheaded in Viking days; from 1658, the monastery, which was erected at the beginning of the 11th century, was used as a fortress and prison. There are delightful views of the city and fjord from bathing places on the island. *Ferry every hour from 10am–6pm in summer | return fare 90 NOK | from Ravnkloa dock by the fish hall*

### NIDAROSDOMEN ★

Where can you find Bob Dylan? Walk up the stairs to the top of the ⠵ west tower and you'll see a statue of the Archangel Michael which has an uncanny likeness to the singer and Nobel Prize winner. Enjoy the views over the town before de-

around 1700. *Tue–Sun 10am–4pm | admission 60 NOK | Erling Skakkes gate 47 | www.ntnu.no/vitenskapsmuseet*

## FOOD & DRINK

### AI SUMA
Italian cooking meets upscale Norwegian ingredients in an old granary situated on the prettiest stretch of the River Nidelv. *Kjøpmannsgate 53 | tel. 73 54 92 71 | www.aisuma.no | Moderate*

## SHOPPING

All sorts of bits and pieces and souvenirs are sold in *Røst (Olav Tryggvasons gate 8)* and *Ting (Olav Tryggvasons gate 10)* a paradise for interior design fans. Stylish accessories made of paper and creative ideas to take back home can be found at *Papir & Design (Thomas Angellsgate 22).*

## ENTERTAINMENT

Trondheim attracts a young and relaxed crowd. Start your evening at *Antikvariatet (Nedre Bakklandet 4)* with a beer and a good book. Be sure to stay for the jazz concert later on in the evening. "Kiss the Prince" – if not the real one, then at least try a cocktail with the same name, served at the *Raus Bar (Nordre gate 21).*

## WHERE TO STAY

### CLARION COLLECTION HOTEL BAKERIET
Elegant hotel with light, comfortable rooms, away from traffic but still in the centre. *109 rooms | Brattørgata 2 | tel. 73 99 10 00 | www.choicehotels.no | Expensive*

### CITY LIVING FRU SCHØLLER
No breakfast at this central old town hotel, but many rooms have kitchenettes. Quiet, simple, clean. *50 rooms | Dronningens gate 26 | tel. 73 87 08 00 | www.cityliving.no | Budget–Moderate*

### SINGSAKER SOMMERHOTELL
The largest wooden residential building in Scandinavia is actually a students' hall of residence. Rooms with one to four beds, some with private shower. *Mid-June–mid-Aug | 103 rooms | Rogertsgate 1 | tel. 73 89 31 00 | sommerhotell.singsaker.no | Budget*

## INFORMATION

*Turistinformasjon (Nordre gate 11 | tel. 73 80 76 60 | www.visittrondheim.no)*

## WHERE TO GO

INSIDER TIP ▶ **DEN GYLNE OMVEG**
**(139 D3)** (*ꝳ D11–12*)
The "Golden Detour" branches off from the E 6 north of Verdal and follows Roads 755 and 761 across the peninsula of *Inderøya*, passing galleries, bakeries and farm shops. If the weather cooperates, go for a cycling tour or head to Trondheimsfjord for some fishing. *www.visitinnherred.com*

# LOW BUDGET

Hikers in north Trøndelag will find cosy cabins at *Føllingstua Camping Site* 14 km/8½ miles north of Steinkjer *(hut for 1–2 people 990 NOK/day | tel. 74 14 71 90 | www.follingstua.no)*

Admission to *Pirbadet (Havnegata 12 | www.pirbadet.no)* in Trondheim costs 115 instead of 155 NOK one hour before closing (Mon–Fri 9pm, Sat/Sun 7pm). Take a quick plunge to leave you fresh and ready for the city's entertainment.

# NORDLAND

**At first glance, what opens up beyond Trondheim is just an endlessly long, narrow stretch of land. But this soon turns out to be one of the most beautiful and varied regions in Norway.**

The narrowest piece of Norway is located in the *fylke* Nordland – it is a mere 6 km/3¾ miles from the end of the Tysfjord to the Swedish border.

Only two roads make their way northwards: one, through a densely forested valley and the other, with the help of numerous ferries, along the coast. If you take the main road to the north, the E6, you will need almost an entire day to drive from the southern border of Nordland to Narvik. So just pull over to the right and let this region – already arctic in character – charm you with all

that it has to offer: nature galore. Nordland is the homeland of Knut Hamsun; this is where the poet and Nobel Prize laureate created and settled many of the characters in his books. They live from fishing and love their Nordland, cheerful stories and crude jokes. The Nordlanders are always full of respect when they talk about the weather and do not let themselves be put down by the whims of nature or by the high and mighty. It will also not take you very long to find out just how warm-hearted the people here can be.

Although Nordland is small, it is big enough for many a holiday and a trip with the Hurtigruten ships along the coast of Helgeland is the beginning of an intense relationship for many. Alpine lakes lie hidden behind the boulders of the eastern

Tarry awhile: a small strip of land, hospitable people and an incredibly beautiful mass of islands

Saltfjell Mountains and there are massive glaciers with gigantic grottos beneath them – some even accessible *(www.nordlandsnaturen.no)*. Knut Hamsun's country is the north of the *fylke* between Bodø and Narvik: a paradise on the coast. Offshore lie the Lofoten Islands – they are so unique that there is a special chapter devoted to them in this guide.

People who visit a Nordland island far out at sea are always given a warm welcome and can take an active part in the daily lives of the fishermen and fish farmers. The landscape and the atmosphere "way out here" are the perfect framework for a dream holiday on the Norwegian Sea.

# BODØ

**(140 B4)** *(Ø F8)* **Sharp tongues claim that it is always windy in Bodø (pop. 50,000). It must be said that this harbour town and Nordland's capital does indeed lie open to the Vestfjord.**

Bodø: Feel the wind in your hair at the Nyholmen entrenchment

Only the 800 m (2,600 ft) high rugged peaks on Landego Island off the coast provide a little protection from the icy storms from the north west.

Bodø received its town charter in 1860 but the German attack on 27 May 1940 destroyed the entire built-up area. That is why, today, many visitors think Bodø seems rather boring; there are not many buildings or residential areas worth seeing. But the people living in Bodø make up for that: when you take a stroll over the Moloveien on the sea-shore you will soon recognise that the Bodøværinger are warm-hearted and open-minded – their good humour typifies the town.

Bodø is also major a traffic junction. This is the terminus of the Nordland railway and the Hurtigruten ships dock directly opposite the station. This is where many holiday-makers take a ferry to the Lofoten. Express ships set off for the remote regions and islands on both sides of Vestfjord. This is also the nursery of the Northern-Atlantic cod and if you want to eat a delicious dish of this fish, Bodø is the right place to do so.

## SIGHTSEEING

### BODIN KIRKE

The stone church, built around 1240, lies directly on Saltfjord about 3 km/1.8 mile from the town centre. The richly deco-rated altarpiece from 1670 is especially noteworthy. The "Baroque organ" is younger by contrast as it is a replica that was made in 2003 but its sound is none-theless impressive. *Mid-June–late Aug Mon–Fri 10am–3pm*

### KEISERVARDEN ☆

An easy, three-hour hike over the near-by hills will be rewarded with the most beautiful view over the Norwegian Sea to the Lofoten Wall. From 350 m/1,150 ft up, just below the treeline, you can watch the midnight sun sink until it barely touches the sea before rising again – provided that the summer weather is fine. Concerts are also held here during the *Nordland Music Festival*. *More information and hiking maps are available at the Tourist Information Office*

## NORDLANDSMUSEET BODØ

The everyday life of Nordland's fish farmers and the Sami settlements are the main subjects in the oldest building in Nordland (built in 1903). Bodø's iron-age silver treasure, which was found in 1919, is also kept here. *June–Aug daily 11am–5pm, Sat/Sun 11am–4pm, otherwise Mon–Fri 9am–3pm | admission 60 NOK | Prinsensgate 116 | www.nordlandsmuseet.no/ nordlandsmuseet*

## NORSK LUFTFARTSMUSEUM

The history of Norwegian civil aviation and the air force, a flight simulator and the depiction of what happens when a plane takes off or lands: exciting impressions for young and old. *June–Aug daily 10am–7pm, otherwise Mon–Fri 10am–4pm, Sat/Sun 11am–5pm | admission 160 NOK | www.luftfart.museum.no*

## NYHOLMEN KULTURHISTORISK OMRÅDE (LIGHTHOUSE AND ENTRENCHMENT) ⚓

The reconstructed entrenchment that protected the trading station at Hundholmen, the later town of Bodø, between 1810 and 1835 is located on a small island just offshore from the town. If you walk to the lighthouse, you will have a fine view of Bodø and the surrounding area from the sea.

## FOOD & DRINK

### HJERTEROMMET ●

Behind the creaking, red door hides a real gem. This café exudes warmth and cosiness with its shabby yet charming floor, tables and chairs. Treat yourself to the speciality crêpe traditionally served with *brunost* cheese. *Gamle Riksvei 51 | tel. 75 53 80 45 | Budget–Moderate*

### LØVOLDS KAFETERIA

Reasonably-priced Norwegian home-style cooking. The restaurant swears by products from the Arctic and large portions. If you want to try boiled halibut, this is the place do it! *Tollbugta 9 | tel. 75 52 02 61 | komplettfritid.no/dagens-meny | Budget*

## SHOPPING

Seeing that it is always windy and sometimes quite cold, an entire street of shops in Bodø has been glazed over: you will find everything you need in the *Glashuset*

---

**MARCO POLO HIGHLIGHTS**

★ **Kjerringøy**
Ancient coastal traditions are coming back to life on the peninsula to the north of Bodø → p. 75

★ **Saltstraumen**
Unbelievable power: the fastest tidal river in Norway is a terrifyingly beautiful natural phenomenon → p. 76

★ **Svartisen**
North Norway's largest glacier reaches down to the sea, protects the hinterland from storms and conceals many secrets within it → p. 76

in the centre. Souvenirs, jewellery and useful articles made of (mostly local) stone, can be bought at *Bertnes Geo-Senter (www.bertnesgeosenter.no | around 8 km/5 miles east of Bodø)*.

## SPORTS & ACTIVITIES

### FISHING
Fishing is possible everywhere here. In the fjord and on the open sea, from the shore or a boat. Salmon, cod and halibut of seemingly record size can be caught on the *cutter trips on the Saltstraumen*. The size of the boat, length of the excursion and price vary according to the number of people taking part. *Info: Tuvsjyen AS (tel. 75 58 77 91 | www.tuvsjyen.com)*

### NORDLANDSBADET ●
One of the loveliest water parks in Norway. Various swimming pools and slides, whirlpools and corners where you can relax – and a *spa area (Mon–Thu 3pm–9pm, Fri/Sat noon-8pm, Sun until 6pm / admission 230–270 NOK)* with grottos, a herbal steam bath and Finnish sauna on the first floor. *Mon–Fri 3pm–9pm (Tue, Fri from 6:30am), Sat/Sun 10am–6pm | admission 150 (weekends 170) NOK | Plassmyrveien 11–15 | www.bodospektrum.no*

### SEA EAGLE SAFARI
In the summer, *Stella Polaris* organize a daily trip at 4pm to the island of *Landego* to see Scandinavia's largest bird of prey in action. *Ferry 650 NOK | book at the Tourist Information Office | departure from the Hurtigruten dock*

## WHERE TO STAY

It is worth going to the Tourist Information Office before choosing where to spend the night. They have a daily listing of reasonably-priced vacancies.

### BODØ VANDRERHJEM
Spending the night in a railway station that is still the last stop of the Nordland railway is something different, and very international to boot! Breakfast, which is included in the price, is served in *Café Diplomat* on the second floor. *21 rooms (73 beds) | Sjøgata 57 | tel. 75 50 80 48 | www.hihostels.no/bodo | Moderate*

### SALTSTRAUMEN HOTEL & CAMPING
Idyllic hotel 35 km/21¾ miles from Bodø on Road 17 in the midst of wonderful scenery directly on the tidal River Saltstraumen. Cosy cabins, good Norwegian cooking. Sauna and bathtubs

# DARK DAYS, BRIGHT NIGHTS

Ever heard of the invention called the daylight lamp? No? Well you could need one above the polar circle when daylight is scarce in the winter months. Artificial lighting could stop you getting the blues and from falling into the classic winter depression. The opposite is true in summer when sunlight is in abundance and the sun never real-ly goes down the further north you go. Once you have crossed the polar circle, you have every chance of witnessing the midnight sun. The light sky will play havoc with your biorhythm, causing some people to survive off less sleep and leaving others feeling fitter and healthier. A barbecue in the special light of this night sun is a truly unique experience.

Anything else? Traditional grocer's store in Kjerringøy

outside in the fresh air. *28 rooms, 12 cabins | Saltstraumen | tel. 75 50 65 60 | www.satstraumenhotell.no | Moderate*

## SKAGEN HOTEL

This hotel, where the breakfast chef conjures up delicious dishes requested by the guests and keeps everybody happy, is tastefully decorated and – in spite of its central location – very peaceful. *71 rooms | Nyholmsgata 11 | tel. 75 51 91 00 | www.skagen-hotel.no | Expensive*

## INFORMATION

*Turistinformasjon (Sentrumsterminalen | tel. 75 54 80 00 | www.visitbodo.com)*

## WHERE TO GO

### KJERRINGØY ★ (140 C4) (*Ⅲ F7*)

Traditional trading post with 15 buildings from the 19th century in an absolutely beautiful coastal setting. Here you will get a good impression of the everyday life led by the masters and their servants in a typical Norwegian merchant town in times gone by – almost just like in one of Knut Hamsun's novels The café ☻ INSIDERTIP *Markens Grøde (late July– late Aug)* only uses products from neighbouring Kjerringøy organic farm. A hike from the Kjerringøy parsonage to ☝ *Middagshaugen* mountain is worthwhile (don't forget to put on your hiking boots). *Late May–late Aug daily 11am– 5pm, May & Sept only Sat/Sun noon– 4pm | admission 110 NOK | ordlandsmuseet.no/kjerringoy_handelssted | 38 km/24 miles north of Bodø on Road 834*

### RØST AND VÆRØY (140 A4) (*ⅢE7*)

You can reach these bird islands either in the 35-seat plane operated by Widerøe or by ferry from Bodø. The approximately 1,300 people who have their home on these islands live from fish. The constant

The Saltstraumen is Norway's most powerful tidal river

*Røst is 100 km/63 miles from Bodø (the ferry takes around 7 hours), Værøy 85 km/54 miles (around 4.5 hours)*

### SALTSTRAUMEN ★ (140 B4) (*ⓜ F8*)

The most savage tidal river in the country is even a gruesomely beautiful sight from far away. Within a mere 6 hours, masses of water are forced through the 3 km (1.9 mile) long and only 150 m (492 ft) wide sound at almost 40 km/h – you can even hear the thundering force of nature from the bridge. Fishermen appreciate other qualities that this fjord entrance has to offer: this is where the largest rock salmon in Europe are caught, the record is 22.7 kg (50 lb). If you want to experience the force of the current close up, you can hire a good boat for a fishing trip at *Saltstraumen Brygge (tel. 92 45 51 00 | www.sfc.no | 1100 NOK per day)* and book accommodation (flats and cabins, *Budget–Moderate*). *33 km/20½ miles east of Bodø*

### SULITJELMA (140 C4) (*ⓜ F8*)

The former mining town of Sulitjelma, where copper was extracted between 1887 and 1991, lies at the end of Road 830, surrounded by mountain ranges and glaciers. The *Mining Museum (in summer, daily 11am–5pm | admission 60 NOK)* gives an overview of 100 years of mining. *106 km/66 miles east of Bodø*

### SVARTISEN ★ (140 B5) (*ⓜ E–F 8–9*)

You can get very close to Norway's second-largest glacier if you approach it from the sea. *Engabreen*, a glacier snout that reaches down to the shore, is an especially popular tourist destination. In summer, small ships depart daily from the village of *Holand (170 km/106 miles from Bodø | on Road 17)* for the glacier; visitors have to walk the last 3 km/1.8 mile to the ice on the path or rent a bicy-

wind, mild winters and cool summers make it the perfect place for producing dried cod that is then exported to southern Europe. The cliffs on the south-west of the island provide shelter for gigantic colonies of seabirds. A quarter of Norway's entire seabird population nests on the rocks of Røst – and that means around 2.5 million birds: puffins, gulls, cormorants and sea eagles. The tourist offices on the islands can give further information on boat trips to the bird rocks.

cle (rentals at the dock). Equipment for climbing the glacier is available on site. *Info and bookings for glacier tours at Rocks 'n Rivers (May–Sept | 900 NOK for 6 hours | tel. 41 08 29 81 | www.rocks nrivers.no).*

INSIDER TIP ▶ TRÆNA (140 A5) *(Ⓜ E9)*
There are good reasons for visiting northern Norway's smallest community (pop. 500). Only very few of the almost 1,000 islands and islets near the Arctic Circle are inhabited, and the people here have all grown up with the sea. They are fishermen or involved in salmon farming and happy to see any visitor who comes by. Even hobby anglers will be very successful in the fishing grounds between the islands, and the enormous puffin colony on the island of *Lovund* is a fascinating spectacle. At the beginning of July, the *Træna Festival (3-day pass 1,500 NOK | www.trena.net)* takes place: first-rate rock and pop from Norway, around 2,000 – mostly young – visitors, tent camps, fine seafood

straight off the cutter, sun and rain are the ingredients that make this an unforgettable experience at the Arctic Circle. Accommodation is available in the *Træna Rorbuferie* fishing huts *(tel. 97 98 32 76 | www.rorbuferie.com | Budget)* on Husøy. *140 km/88 miles from Bodø | express ship from Bodø or Sandnessjøen/Nesna/Stokkvågen (same ship)*

# NARVIK

(141 D3) *(Ⓜ G6)* **Some of the fiercest battles in World War II were fought in Narvik (pop. 22,500). The reason was the harbour's economic and strategic importance.**
Iron ore from the mines in Kiruna in Sweden is still shipped out of Narvik today. The gigantic loading wharfs are the first and most dominating impression of a town that is located in a magnificent setting.

# FOR BOOKWORMS & FILM BUFFS

**My Struggle** – in six volumes (A Death In the Family, A Man In Love, Boyhood Island, Dancing In the Dark, Some Rain Must Fall, The End) by Karl Ove Knausgård is an autobiographical account of the writer's life and an amazing piece of contemporary literature. The question is not if you should read it, but when...

**The Snowman** – (2007) is a novel by the star Norwegian crime writer Jo Nesbø packed with suspense and eeriness. After reading it, you'll see Oslo from a completely different perspective...

**Here Is Harold** – Harold (Bjørn Sundquist) feels cheated in life and for revenge plans to kidnap the famous Ikea founder Ingvar Kamprad. His amateurish attempts are portrayed in this dark comedy (2016, director: Gunnar Vikene)

**Trollhunter** – Anybody who believed that there were no trolls in Norway was shown that this is not true in this film (2011), directed by André Øvredal. This parody on the gnarled giants can make you shudder a little – and laugh a lot.

## SIGHTSEEING

### FJELLHEISEN (CABLE CAR) ☼

If you decide to stay in town but still want to have a fine view, the cable car *(fjell-heisen)* can be recommended – it will whisk you up to an elevation of 656 m/2,100 ft in a mere seven minutes. When the sky is blue, the fjord and fjell – and sometimes the midnight sun – combine to create a breathtaking panorama. *June–20 July daily 1pm–1am, 21 July–20 Aug 1pm–10pm | fare 180 NOK*

### NORDLAND RØDE KORS KRIGSMINNENMUSEUM

The battles for Narvik and its iron ore as well as the destruction of the town in World War II are documented in this museum. The exhibition is well worth seeing and thought provoking. *In summer Mon–Sat 10am–4pm, Sun noon–4pm | admission 100 NOK | an the Market Square | www.warmuseum.no*

### INSIDER TIP OFOTBANEN ☼

The Ofot Railway, one of the most exciting stretches of track in Europe, runs between fjords and Arctic plateaus. Travelling on this train will give you an idea of the hardships the migrant workers who built the line more than 100 years ago had to endure. *Visit Narvik (see "Information")* offers guided round-trip tours *(late June–late Aug | 600 NOK)*. Head by train to Katterat up in the mountains, then hike 13 km/8 miles to Rombaksbotn at the end of the fjord with the same name where an RIB boat will pick you up.

## FOOD & DRINK

### RALLAR'N PUB OG KRO

Rustic and somewhat loud in the evenings thanks to the live music, but still a place to get a solid meal at lunchtime. *Kongensgate 64 | in Quality Hotel Grand Royal | tel. 76 97 70 00 | www.nordichoice hotels.no | Moderate*

## SPORTS & ACTIVITIES

Alpine sports are very popular between the fjord and fjell: World Cup races are even held in Narvik. The cable cars and lifts operate until late May. The ski centre is right in town making distances between your accommodation and the slopes short. Narvik after a fresh snowfall is a favourite among snowboarders.

## WHERE TO STAY

### BREIDABLIKK GJESTEHUS ☼

Simple, but very cosy and centrally located with a fantastic view of the city and

## LOW BUDGET

Island-hopping by bicycle will make it easy for you to discover the island and skerry paradise along Helgeland's coast and also bring you closer to the culture and people. Tips for routes and maps plus bikes can be obtained at the tourist information offices in Sandnessjøen and Brønnøysund. *245 NOK per day (incl. helmet) | tel. 75 01 80 00 | www.visithelgeland.com*

The fjell farm *Furuheim Gård* in Susendal provides fresh produce straight from the field, overnight stays in untamed natural surroundings, culture and plenty of other activities. (*Overnight stay 300 NOK per person, breakfast and supper 50 NOK per meal | Hattfjeelldal | tel. 92 84 83 56 | www.furuheimgaard.no*

Swaying above Narvik in a cable car is particularly beautiful when the weather is good

its surroundings. An oasis in summer. *21 rooms | Tore Hundsgate 41 | tel. 76 94 14 18 | breidablikk.no | Moderate*

### NORUMGÅRDEN BED & BREAKFAST

Magnificent wooden villa in a suburb a bit out of the centre; decorated with antiques and beautifully furnished rooms. *4 rooms | Framnesvei 127 | tel. 76 94 48 57 | Budget*

### INFORMATION

*Turistinformasjon | Visit Narvik (Stasjonsveien 1 | tel. 76 96 56 00 | www. visitnarvik.com)*

### WHERE TO GO

**HAMARØY (140 C3) (ΜΟ F7)**
"The sky all open and clean; I stared into that clear sea,...". This sentence in Knut Hamsun's book *Pan* was written during the many years he spent on the Hamarøy Peninsula. The community lies in a picturesque coastal setting among bizarre peaks. The *Hamsunsenteret (early June–mid-Aug daily 11am–6pm, otherwise shorter opening hours | admission 110 NOK | Presteid | www.hamsunsenteret. no)* created by the American architect Steven Holl shows the most comprehensive exhibition on the life and work of the famous novelist anywhere. Spend the night in the lighthouse *Tranøy fyr (15 rooms | tel. 99 70 44 99 | www.tranoyfyr. no | Moderate)*, where you will fall asleep with the tang of salt on your lips and the shriek of seagulls in your ears. This is also a place where anglers will be able to reel in some impressive cod. *100 km/62 miles south of Narvik*

# LOFOTEN

**Even getting there is an experience: no matter whether you come by ferry or plane from the mainland, you can't miss the massive Lofoten Wall – an endless row of jagged peaks that rise up out of Vestfjord.**

Many fishing villages lie between these peaks while small towns, farms and historical treasure troves are hidden in the hinterland. The Lofoten archipelago stretches 150 km/93 miles northwards along the west side of Vestfjord.

The *car ferry* departs from Bodø for Moskenes *(around 3½ hours)* or from Skutvik for Svolvær *(2 hours)*. You can reach Svolvær by catamaran from Bodø *(departures Mon–Thu, Sat 5:15pm, Fri 6pm, Sun 8:30pm | travel time around 3.5 hours | no cars! | www.thn.no)*.

The "overland route", with many bridges and a short ferry crossing, is the E10 from Narvik as far as Å, the southernmost point of the island group directly next to the Moskenes ferry wharf – a trip that takes in all of the main islands of the Lofoten.

Anybody who visits the Lofoten should spend at least one night in a *rorbu*. For almost 1,000 years, these houses built on piles in the water were where the fishermen lived during the fishing season. The modern versions are robust and still dressed in seaweed washed in by the waves, but they are outfitted very differently (booking at Destination Lofoten in Svolvær).

Alpine peaks and the depths of the ocean: fishing is important, but it is mainly tourism that breathes life into this group of islands

# LEKNES

(140 B3) *(𝄢 E7)* **As is the case with all of the other larger towns on the Lofoten, Leknes (pop. 3,200) is not especially attractive.**

Leknes is the centre of the island and community of Vestvågøy and has an important airport. The post-war architecture has no charm at all but the surroundings of the small town have a lot to offer.

SIGHTSEEING

### LOFOTR VIKING MUSEUM ★

This is how the ancestors of the Norwegians lived: the museum to the north of Leknes has an impressive reconstruction of the largest Viking house ever found (83 m/272 ft long). The Vikings held political and religious meetings in the "guildhall". *June–mid-Aug daily 10am–7pm, otherwise shorter opening hours | admission 200 NOK | www.lofotr. no*

Scent of the sea: typical fish drying system on Moskenes

## FOOD & DRINK

### SKJÆBRYGGA
Excellent fish dishes are served here directly on the quay in Stamsund, 15 km/ 9¼ miles east of Leknes. *Tel. 76 05 46 00 | www.skjaebrygga.no | Moderate*

## SHOPPING

### LOFOTEN DESIGN
15 km/9 miles south of Leknes turn to the right towards the Sea. There in the village of Vikten lies Åse and Åsvar Tangrand's glass blowing and pottery workshop. The two artists give their imagination free rein – much to the delight of the visitors. *June–Aug daily 10am–7pm | admission to the workshop and "Potter's Tower" 20 NOK | www.glasshyttavikten.no*

## WHERE TO STAY

### BRUSTRANDA SJØCAMPING ☆
An amazing view, refreshing sea air and cosy cabins on the water. *18 cabins (2–6 people) | 17 km/10.5 miles north-east of Leknes on Road 815 | tel. 90 47 36 30 | www.brustranda.no | Budget–Moderate*

## INFORMATION

Destination Lofoten (Sentrum | tel. 76 08 75 53 | www.lofoten.info)

# REINE

(140 B3) *(Ɱ E7)* ☆ Reine is picturesque in the true sense of the word. Generations of landscape painters and photographers have come to the main town on the southern-most Lofoten island Moskenes (pop. 1,100) to capture their impressions of the contrasts in the scenery that range from pointed mountain peaks to pretty villages and clear water.

There is the smell of fish drying on the racks typical of the Lofoten everywhere here from March to autumn. Some of the most beautiful viewpoints and fishing villages in the Lofoten are in this area.

## SIGHTSEEING

### FLAKSTAD KIRKE ★

This simple wooden church was once built from cargo driftwood and resembles a ship itself. The model of a fishing boat in the centre of the church reminds visitors of the community's maritime roots.

### INSIDER TIP ► LOFOTEN TØRRFISKMUSEUM

Å is a living museum village. The production of dried fish has a long tradition on the Lofoten and that is shown here in the buildings of a traditional fish factory. Accommodation in the village *(www.lofotenferie.com). June–late Aug Mon–Sat 11am–5pm, otherwise by appointment | admission 60 NOK | end of the E10*

### MOSKENESTRAUMEN

The strait lies between the southern tip of the Lofoten, Lofotodden, and the island of Værøy. There are guided walks to the legendary maelstrom, made famous by Edgar Allan Poe, in summer.

### NUSFJORD

The fishing village on the Vestfjord has been a Unesco World Heritage site since 1975. Most of the *rorbuer* date from the 19th century and have been restored and turned into holiday accommodation. *www.nusfjord.no | south on the E10, turn left after Kilan*

### SAKRISØY

The more than 100-year-old, red and white huts in this fishing settlement form a fantastic contrast to the surrounding mountains. Where to stay: *Buene på Valen (tel. 90 06 15 66 | www. sakrisoy.no/buene.htm | Moderate | 3.5 km/2 miles north on the E10).*

## FOOD & DRINK

### RAMBERG GJESTEGÅRD

Here you will be served Lofoten Island lamb as well as fish and even whale meat. There is also a beach of fine sand and ten dwellings. *Ramberg | tel. 76 09 35 00 | www.ramberg-gjestegard. no | Moderate*

## SPORTS & ACTIVITIES

Bicycles and boats are available for rent at almost all places to stay. You can fish from the shore or from a boat.

## WHERE TO STAY

### MAREN ANNA

This guesthouse in Sørvågen lies directly on the water, the rooms with a view are cosy and bright, the speciality of the restaurant *(Moderate)* is rock salmon roasted with lemon. *11 rooms | tel. 76 09 20 50 | www.marenanna.no | Budget*

---

**MARCO POLO HIGHLIGHTS**

★ **Lofotr Viking Museum**
The way the forefathers of the Norwegians lived: a replica of an 83-metre-long house from Viking times has been built on the island of Vestvågøy → p. 81

★ **Flakstad Kirke**
The dazzlingly red church is the most beautiful house of worship on the Lofoten → p. 83

★ **Trollfjord**
A fairy-tale fjord arm – and so narrow that big ships can hardly turn around → p. 84

*Turistkontoret Flakstad & Moskenes (Moskenes ferry wharf | tel. 98 01 75 64 | tour-ff@lofoten-info.no)*

# SVOLVÆR

**(140 B3) (*ℳ F7*) The capital of the Lofoten lies beneath the Svolvægeita Mountain (Solvær Goat); it has this name because its two peaks resemble horns.**
The value of the landed cod, herrings and farmed salmon makes Solvær (pop. 4,500) one of the most important fishing ports in northern Norway. The racks used for drying fish around the town centre, which can also be seen on the smaller islands, are clear evidence of this.

## SIGHTSEEING

### LOFOTMUSEET
The regional museum was established on the remains of Vågar, the only northern Norwegian town in the Middle Ages. The main building is a grand merchant's house from 1815; the everyday life of simple people is the main focus of the exhibition in the other houses. And, of course, fishing and cargo boats make up most of the exhibits. The 2 km/1¼ mile long path, "The First Town in the North", leads you to seven cultural monuments. *In summer daily 10am–6pm, otherwise shorter opening hours | admission 90 NOK | Storvågen (part of Kabelvåg) | www. lofotmuseet.no*

### TROLLFJORD ⭐
Experience the monumental natural beauty of the Trollfjord. Large tourist ships have to turn around in this extremely narrow side-arm of Raftsund. While this is happening, passengers admire the rocky shore rising straight up to the skies and the fascinating play of light on the water. *June–Aug several trips on the fjord (2½–4 hours) | tickets from Destination Lofoten*

## FOOD & DRINK

### BØRSEN SPISERI
The maritime restaurant (reservations advisable) is associated with the 30 *rorbuer* that can accommodate two to six guests at *Svinøya Rorbuer. Gunnars Bergs vei 2 | tel. 76 06 99 301| www.svinoya.no | Moderate*

## SHOPPING

### SKANDINAVISK HØYFJELLSUTSTYR
In case you forget something you need for your trekking holiday: the experts in this shop not only know everything about the land and water in the vicinity, they can also provide you with the all the necessary equipment. *Håkon Kyllingsmarks gate 3*

## LOW BUDGET

The *Munkebu cabin (www.turistfore ningen.no)* lies in the Djupfjordheia highlands not far from Sørvågen, and *Selfjordhytta (www.lofoten-turlag.no)* on the picturesque Selfjord near Flakstad. Bring your own bed linens and food! Many hiking possibilities. *15 beds | 250 NOK per person*

*Vikingmarked (6–10 Aug | www.lafotr. no):* The Viking Days at the Viking Centre in Borg feature handicrafts, games, lectures and music just like 1,000 years ago. Admission is free!

## SPORTS & ACTIVITIES

### FISHING

In summer, cutters and tourist ships take hobby anglers out to sea. Anybody can participate in the *World Cod Fishing Championship* at the end of March. *More information from Destination Lofoten*

### INSIDER TIP KAISER ROUTE

From Svolvær through the countryside of the northern Lofoten: the 220-km-long (136 miles) Kaiser route will take you to remote places that are hardly ever reached by car – along Raftsund with world-famous Trollfjord and back

true. Experience the open sea and the jagged mountain peaks even more intensely in the light of the midnight sun. Reservations advisable. *Lofoten Opplevelser | tel. 90 58 14 75 | www.lofoten-opplevelser.no*

## WHERE TO STAY

### SCANDIC SVOLVÆR

This modern hotel lies in perfect harmony with nature on a small island in the harbour. *146 rooms | tel. 76 07 22 22 | www.scandichotels.com | Expensive*

Observe the mighty sea eagles in their natural habitat on the Lofoten

to the start. Cycling is most enjoyable in the evening. If you are lucky, harbour porpoises or even killer whales might accompany you on your way through Raftsund.

### SEAL AND SEA EAGLE SAFARI

Sea eagle and seal safaris (1.5 hours) with a solid RIB boat depart from Henningsvær (650 NOK). If the weather is good, the INSIDER TIP three-hour midnight tours to the western side of the Lofoten (900 NOK) is a dream come

### SVOLVÆR SJØHUSCAMPING

The atmosphere in this house on the quay only a few minutes from the centre of town is rustically maritime and cosy. Rooms with two or four beds, as well as a holiday flat, are available. *13 rooms | Parkgata 12 | tel. 76 07 03 36 | www.svolver-sjohuscamping.no | Budget*

## INFORMATION

*Destination Lofoten (Torget | tel. 76 06 98 00 | www.lofoten.info)*

# TROMS

Welcome to Troms in Arctic Europe where the treeline sinks lower and the mountain ranges towering out of the ocean become more barren.

The scenery at the foot of the mountains is full of gems: sandy beaches and old fishing villages on the islands plus rivers full of fish and broad valleys in the interior. However, you will only be able to enjoy the stable summer weather protected by a mosquito net.

Tourism on Svalbard profits from the natural scenery of the Arctic and the history of the island group as a whaling and sealing station. Large areas are protected and outdoor activities strictly regulated. The "Land of the Pointed Mountains", as it was called by its discoverer Willem Barents in 1596, cannot sustain mass tourism.

# SVALBARD (SPITS-BERGEN)

(138 A–B 1–2) (⌖ N–O1) Ice-capped mountains with glaciers on their slopes running into the sea, high mountain valleys that are only free of snow in the west and at the height of summer; but ★ Svalbard, the "Land of the Cold Coasts", is not an icy desert.

What attracts increasingly more tourists to Svalbard? Is it the absolute peace and tranquillity or the fresh, bitingly cold air? The thrill of suddenly encountering a polar bear could also be another reason.

Cold shores and green islands: the breadth of the north from the university town of Tromsø to the "Land of the Pointed Mountains"

Local inhabitants always carry a weapon just in case. A safer option is to take a guided tour, for example by snowmobile or in a kayak in between ice floes on the fjords.

## FOOD & DRINK

### FRUENE
Fresh bread and pastries, lunches, various types of coffee and unique praline creations to take home. *Lompensenteret | tel. 79 02 76 40 | Moderate*

## WHERE TO STAY

**INSIDER TIP COALMINERS' CABIN**
Stay the night at a reasonable price where the coal miners used to live – on the outskirts of town and below the mountains and glaciers. Meals are still served in the "main mess hall" that is a meeting place for guests from all over the world with one thing in common: they all want to discover Svalbard. *73 rooms | Vei 100–6 | tel. 79 02 63 00 | www.spitsbergentravel.no | Budget–Moderate*

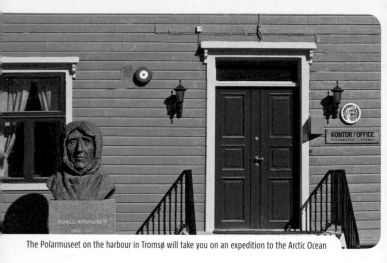

The Polarmuseet on the harbour in Tromsø will take you on an expedition to the Arctic Ocean

### FUNKEN LODGE ☙

Another old building from the coal mining company. No soot on the walls just an authentic miner's ambience full of warmth and cosiness.*88 rooms | tel. 79 02 62 00 | www.spitsbergentravel.no | Expensive*

## INFORMATION

*Svalbard Reiseliv (Longyearbyen | tel. 79 02 55 50 | visitsvalbard.com)*

# TROMSØ

**(141 D1) (*ð G5*) A "cool" city! ★ Tromsø (pop. 75,000) is a vibrant light illuminating the country's dark north.**

Boasting a lively music scene and animated pub culture, the city's nightlife attracts a predominately young crowd of students from the world's most northern university. The city can stay covered in snow until mid-May, shortly after which the midnight sun appears between 23 May and 23 July. Enjoy spending the long nights sat beneath starry skies – just be prepared to pack up warm.

## SIGHTSEEING

### FJELLHEISEN (CABLE CAR) ☙

The cable cars, known as "seal" and "polar bear", take you up to the top of Mount Storsteinen (421 m/1,380 ft) in just four minutes. The views of the city and the mouth of the polar sea will literally take your breath away. *Daily every half hour, winter 10am–10pm, summer 10am–1am | 170 NOK | www.fjellheisen.no*

### ISHAVSKATEDRALEN

The glass "Arctic Ocean Cathedral" can be spotted from the city centre – the best way to get there is to walk across the ☙ city bridge (Tromsø bru). The gigantic glass mosaic on the east wall is especially impressive as are the *Midnight Sun Concerts (daily from 11pm | 170 NOK)* – the organ sounds and acoustics are amazing. *May–Aug Mon–Sat 9am–7pm, Sun 1pm–7pm | admission 50 NOK | www.ishavskatedralen.no*

### PERSPEKTIVET MUSEUM

How difficult was life here on the edge of the Arctic circle, how important was fishing or how did the traders live? The exhibits in this listed building will help you answer these questions and come to a better understanding of northern Norway. *Tue–Sun 11am–5pm | free admission | Storgata 95 | www.perspektivet.no*

### POLARMUSEET

Norway's polar history, expeditions and seal and polar bear hunting are the themes in the Polar Museum that has been set up between the old harbour warehouses. *In summer daily 10am–7pm, otherwise shorter opening hours | admission 50 NOK | Søndre Tollbodgata 11 | www.polarmuseum.no*

## FOOD & DRINK

### EMMAS DRØMMEKJØKKEN

Emma's real name is Anne Brit. She serves an authentic and legendary fish gratin. Once you have tried the dish, you can cook it by following the recipe online. *Kirkegata 8 | tel. 77 63 77 30 | www.emmasdrommekjokken.no | Moderate*

### SKARVEN

The perfect place for a long, pleasant evening. It can begin in the *Biffhuset (Moderate)* steak restaurant or in the *Arctandria (Expensive)* fish restaurant, continue in the *Kroa (Budget)* pub and finish up in the cocktail bar in the basement. *Strandtorget 1 | tel. 77 60 07 20 | www.skarven.no*

## SHOPPING

The light of the north really makes itself felt in the artistic products created in the *Blåst* glass blowing workshop *(Peder Hansensgate 4 | www.blaast.no)*. Wabi Sabi (Peder Hansens gate 4B | www.wabisabi.no) makes delightful items of jewellery in raw Scandinavian style. The wool, sold in *Snarby Strikkestudio (Fredrik Langes gate 18)* from Raumaull, Sandnes Garn and Hillesvåg wool factory, is also a favourite of Tromsø-born fashion designer Nina Skarra, who now works in New York.

## LEISURE & SPORTS

Husky or reindeer sleigh rides, whale spotting safaris, Northern Lights expeditions or snowboarding tours are once-in- a-lifetime experiences and can be booked online at *www.lyngsfjord.com*. In the *Tromsø Arctic Reindeer Senter (30 minutes from the centre | www.tromsoarcticreindeer.com)* you can trace the lives of the indigenous Sami people.

## ENTERTAINMENT

### BLÅ ROCK CAFÉ

Occasional live bands; DJs on Sun. Happy hour is Mon from 10:30pm–2am. *Strandgata 14–16 | www.facebook.com/Blaarock*

---

★ **Svalbard (Spitsbergen)**
Norway's arctic outpost
→ p. 86

★ **Tromsø**
Party feeling and midnight sun: Nobody wants to go to bed here in summer → p. 88

★ **Lyngsalpen**
Off-piste ski tours in a magical snow scenery → p. 90

★ **Andenes**
Sandy beaches, the open Norwegian Sea and enormous sperm whales → p. 91

**MARCO POLO HIGHLIGHTS**

**ØLHALLEN PUB**

Beer lovers have 67 varieties to choose from in the city's oldest pub. Definitely try *Mack Øl,* the only beer brewed in Tromsø. *Storgata 4 | www.mack.no/ olhallen*

## WHERE TO STAY

**INSIDERTIP ▶ BED & BOOKS**

The "Fisherman's Home" sits on the water, but the "Writer's Home" is somewhat closer to town. Guest share a bathroom and common rooms – experience Norwegian hospitality with an international touch. *9 rooms | Strandveien 45 & 84 | tel. 77 02 98 00 | www.bedandbooks. no | in summer Budget, in winter Moderate*

**SCANDIC ISHAVSHOTEL**

Its location and ship shape make this hotel impossible to miss. If you don't like carpets in strong colours, ask for a room *uten gulvbelleg* (without a carpet). *214 rooms | Frederik Langesgat 2 | on the sound | tel. 77 66 64 00 | www.scandicho tels.com | Expensive*

# LOW BUDGET

The youth hostel ☀ *Tromsø Vandrerhjem* lies in the hills 15 minutes from the town centre *(2 people from 510 NOK | Asgårdveien 9 | tel. 77 65 76 28 | tromsohostell@vand rerhjem.no).*

Experience nature in the fjell and on the coast in 22 self-catering cabins, such as *Senjabu (3 rooms | 250 NOK per person | tel. 77 68 51 75 | www.turist foreningen.no/troms |35 km/22 miles from Finnsnes on Senja island).*

## INFORMATION

*Destinasjon Tromsø (Kirkegata 2 | tel. 77 61 00 00 | www.visittromso.no)*

## WHERE TO GO

### LYNGSALPEN ★ (141 E1) *(₥ H5)*

Lying on the same latitude as Alaska and Greenland, Lyngsalpen offers amazing Arctic alpine scenery and is a magnet for off-slope skiers and extreme sports enthusiasts. *Lyngen Lodge (8 rooms | Olderdalen | tel. 47 62 78 53 | www.lyn genlodge.com | Expensive*) is run by Graham and Elisabeth who ensure the wellbeing of their visitors. *100 km/62 miles westwards on the RV91*

### SOMMARØY (141 D1) *(₥ G5)*

The drive on Road 862 from Tromsø along the south coast of the gigantic *Kvaløya* Island towards the west is an excursion into the fertile agricultural region of Troms and to the beautiful island of Sommarøy. Crystal-clear water, white beaches and flowering front gardens: Many of the locals in Tromsø head here on sunny days for good reason! *80 km/50 miles west of Tromsø*

### VOLLAN GJESTESTUE
**(141 E1–2) *(₥ H5)***

Norway's truck drivers have voted: the best motorway stop in the country is where the E6 and E8 meet. The restaurant serves arctic dishes made with the best-quality ingredients. *22 rooms | tel. 77 72 23 00 | www.vollangjestestue.no | Nordkjosbotn | 70 km/44 miles south of Tromsø | Moderate*

# VESTERÅLEN

**(140 B–C 1–2) *(₥ F5–6)* Part of the Vesterålen island group that continues**

Killer whales are quite at home in the Norwegian Sea

on from the Lofoten in the north belongs to Nordland, but it is best to discover this area from the north.

One of the ways to do this is by taking the small ferry *(June–Aug 3 departures daily)* from *Gryllefjord* **(141 D1)** *(ⓜ G5)* (on the west side of Senja Island) to *Andenes*, the northernmost point of the group of islands. An alternative is to drive on the E10 from *Bjerkvik* **(141 D2)** *(ⓜ G6)*. After 60 km/37.5 miles, head north to *Harstad* or further to the west to *Sortland*. Here, you will have to decide whether you want to go on a whale safari to the northern island of *Andøya* or mountain hiking to *Øksnes* (north-west of Sortland) on the Norwegian Sea.

## SIGHTSEEING

### ANDENES ⭐

Although surrounded by a wall of mountains and snow-white beaches, the main town on the island of Andøya lies at the mercy of the Norwegian Sea. Excursions leave the *Whale Centre (20 June–20 Aug daily 11am, noon, 4pm, 5pm | duration 2–4 hours | from the harbour | 975 NOK, 400 NOK deposit | booking: tel. 76 11 56 00 | www.whalesafari.com)* for the edge of the Norwegian Shelf where sperm

whales up to 18 m (59 ft) regularly show up in summer waiting to be photographed.

### HURTIGRUTEMUSEET STOKMARKNES

Richard With, the "father" of the Hurtigruten, came from Stokmarknes and that is where the *MS Finnmarken* has dropped anchor – as a museum. *Summer daily 10am–6pm | admission 90 NOK | 26 km/16 miles south-west of Sortland on the E10 | www.hurtigrutemuseet.no*

## WHERE TO STAY

### HOTEL MARENA

Hotel with bright and differently decorated rooms in the middle of Andenes, just a stone's throw from the whale centre. *29 rooms | Storgata 15 | tel. 90 08 46 00 | www.hotellmarena.no | Expensive*

## INFORMATION

*Vesterålen Reiseliv (Kjøpmannsgata 2 | Sortland | tel. 76 11 14 80 | www.visit vesteralen.com); Visit Andøy (Kong Hans gate 8 | Andenes | tel. 41 60 58 52 | www. visitandoy.info)*

# FINNMARK

**Icy winds meet open harbours, raging rivers flow into majestic fjords, thousands of peaceful mountain lakes are beleaguered by myriads of mosquitoes.** That is Finnmark: 48,000 km² (18,500 miles²) large and surrounded by the inhospitable coastline of the Arctic Ocean. The interior is characterised by a barren high plateau where tens of thousands of reindeer fight to survive in winter.

The 76,000 people who live in Finnmark have a close relationship to nature that, here, shows all of its facets. Temperatures range from 30°C above to 50°C below zero (+86° to −58°F). In winter, the houses are battered by storms and in summer people bask in the sun on the beautiful sandy beaches and – from time

to time – cool off in the Arctic Ocean; the water can be as warm as 14°C (almost 60°F). In Alta, the midnight sun shines from 16 May to 26 July and even a few days longer at the North Cape.

# ALTA

(142 C3) *(ɰ K2)* **Alta (pop. 20,500) lies on the southern shore of the mighty Altafjord and is the largest town in Finnmark.**
The Fylke's university has been established here and there is also some industry as well as quarries. The Altaelva salmon river flows down from Finnmarksvidda through Alta Canyon before flowing into Altafjord.

The vastness of the Arctic below the North Cape: Barren high plateaus and the Arctic Ocean coastline – Norway's north is full of extremes

## SIGHTSEEING

### ALTA MUSEUM ⭐

What drove the first people to the northern edge of Europe? What did they live from and what did they believe in? The helleristninger, rock drawings up to 7,000 years old, give answers. The 15 km/9.3 mile long prehistoric comic strip includes over 6000 drawings of animals, hunting scenes and ancient legends. The exhibitions on the prehistory of Finnmark are also worth seeing. *Mid-June–late Aug* *daily 8am–8pm, otherwise shorter opening hours | admission 110 NOK| www.alta. museum.no*

## FOOD & DRINK

### DU VERDEN

Rustic, but urban atmosphere: benches lined with reindeer fur and creative Nordic cuisine. Their signature dish is king prawns with chimichurri sauce. *Markedsgata 21 | tel. 45 90 82 13 | www. duverden.no/alta | Moderate–Expensive*

A long and wild hidden beauty: the Alta Canyon

## SPORTS & ACTIVITIES

### ALTA CANYON

It is not easy to find your way to northern Europe's largest canyon, but the effort is worth it. From Gargia Fjellstue (see "Where to Stay"), drive 11 km/7 miles to Sautso and then another 4 km/2.5 miles on the old state road (gravel road). Park your car at the highest point, *Beskades*, and follow the hiking route marked with a red "T" about 7 km/4.3 miles to the end of the 10 km/6.2 miles canyon. Make sure to pack appropriate clothing and mosquito spray! *Description under ut.no/tur/2.6957.*

### HALDDETOPPEN ☼

The hike to the peak of *Haldde Mountain* (904 m/3,000 ft) starts near *Kåfjord* (20 km/12.5 miles to the west of Alta on the E6). In 1898, the first northern-lights observatory was established here. You should be in good shape if you want to make this climb but you will be rewarded with a magnificent view over Altafjord.

## WHERE TO STAY

### GARGIA FJELLSTUE

Rustically decorated bedrooms and public areas. Sami specialities such as snow grouse and cloudberries are served in the restaurant (daily in summer). *13 rooms | tel. 78 43 33 51 | www.gargiafjellstue.no | Moderate*

## INFORMATION

*Alta Bibliotek (Markedsgata 3 | tel. 78 45 58 50 | www.visitalta.no)*

# HAMMERFEST

**(142 C2) (⌀ K1) The most northerly city in the world (pop. 10,500) has existed since 1789.**

Fridtjof Nansen started his expeditions from its ice-free harbour. Today, the gas from the enormous "Snow White" field in the Barents Sea is processed in the refinery in Hammerfest and transported all over the world as liquid gas. The offshore industry provides the whole country with jobs and prosperity.

## SIGHTSEEING

### GJENREISNINGSMUSEET

This museum provides a graphic description of how strongly Hammerfest was affected by World War II and the efforts the Finnmarkingers had to undertake to rebuild it. *In summer daily 10am–4pm, otherwise Mon–Fri 9am–3pm, Sat/Sun 11am–2pm | admission 80 NOK | Kirkegata 21 | www.kystmuseene.no*

### MERIDIAN COLUMN

It is precisely 2,820 km/1,757 miles from this point to the Black Sea – the Meridian line shows you the way. The monument was erected in 1854 to commemorate the first survey of the globe. *In Fuglenes*

## FOOD & DRINK / WHERE TO STAY

### NIRI SUSHI & DINNER

The world's most northerly sushi restaurant serves exciting creations. The signature dish is sushi with reindeer meat. Storgata 22 | tel. 45 50 02 00 | www.niri hammerfest.no | *Moderate–Expensive*

### HOTEL SKYTTERHUSET AS

Situated just seven minutes away from the harbour, this basic and relatively affordable hotel is undergoing extensive renovations but is still open for business as usual. There is a variety of dishes from the buffet for dinner. 145 rooms | *Skytterveien 24 | tel. 78 42 20 10 | www. skytterhuset.no | Moderate*

## SHOPPING

Northern Lights soap and brightly coloured gloves can be found at *Vi4 (Kirkegata 8)*. It's also worth a peek in *Sirkka (Storgata 28)* but it may be worth taking your credit card with you for its tempting jewellery, fashion and interior items.

## INFORMATION

*Turistinformasjon (Hamnegata 3 | tel. 78 41 21 85 | www.hammerfest-turist.no)*

# KARASJOK

(143 D3) (*ØØ L3*) **The community in the middle of Finnmarksvidda has only 2,700 inhabitants but is the political centre of Samiland.**

This is the site of the parliament (Sameting) and extensive Sami collec-

tions. The town is only 18 km/11 miles from the Finnish border and this makes it an important junction on the *Nordkalotte* (North Cape).

## SIGHTSEEING

### KARASJOK GAMLE KIRKE

The Old Church, built in 1807, can be seen from far away; it is the only building in Karasjok that survived World War II. *In summer daily 8am–9pm*

### SAMISK KUNSTNERSENTER

Arts and crafts as well as paintings by Sami artists sold in a bright and peaceful building. *Tue–Fri 10am–4pm, Sat/Sun 11am–4pm | free admission | Suomageaidnu 14 | www.samiskkunstnersenter.no*

## SHOPPING

### BOBLE GLASHYTTE

The northern-most glassworks on earth. The everyday objects are characterised by

★ **Alta Museum**
Primeval petroglyphs in a well-designed museum
→ p. 93

★ **North Cape**
The midnight sun sinking towards the Arctic Sea but hardly touching it creates an indelible impression
→ p. 96

★ **Varanger**
The enormous peninsula in the Arctic Ocean is the epitome of everything that characterises the European Arctic → p. 98

**MARCO POLO HIGHLIGHTS**

their simplicity and subdued colours while the artworks created by the owner Tonje Tunold have much more daring shapes and colours. *Sápmi Park | www. bobleglass.no*

## WHERE TO STAY

### ENGHOLM HUSKY & VANDRERHJEM

Surrounded by forest, sledge dogs and friendly people. Absolutely recommendable: the summer camps in the vastness of Finnmarksvidda (daily excursions or overnight stays). *15 beds | tel. 91 58 66 25 | www.engholm.no | Budget*

## INFORMATION

*Sapmi KS in Scandic Hotel (Porsangerveien 1 | tel. 78 46 88 60 | www.visitsapmi.no)*

# KAUTOKEINO

(142 C4) *(M K3)* **Kautokeino (pop. almost 3,000), the Sami's capital, lies around 130 km/80 miles south of Alta.** Kautokeino has a Sami theatre, Sami university and the Sami major festival is held at Easter *(www.samieasterfestival. com)*

## SIGHTSEEING

### JUHLS' SILVERGALLERY

This silversmith workshop is the life's works of two artists who have united Sami traditions with modern art and attempted to transmit their impressions of the landscapes, myths and people in Finnmark. *In summer daily 9am–8pm, otherwise 9am– 6pm | free tours | www.juhls.no*

### PIKEFOSSEN

45 km/28 miles to the north of Kautokeino and Road 93, this magnificent

waterfall plummets down towards Alta. There is a rest area directly on the road and you can camp near the river.

## FOOD & DRINK / WHERE TO STAY

### THON HOTEL KAUTOKEINO ☾

The only hotel around nestles perfectly into the countryside with its rustic wooden exterior and elegant interior in warm colours. Many rooms have windows with views in two directions. Sami specialities grace the menu of the hotel restaurant *Duottar (Expensive)*. *65 rooms | Biedjovággeluodda 2 | tel. 78 48 70 00 | www. thonhotels.no | Expensive*

## INFORMATION

*Turistinformasjon (in the Sami museum Riddo Duottar | Fefo building | 1st floor | in the Lakselv centre | tel. 40 63 33 86 | www. nordnorge.com)*

# NORTH CAPE

(143 D1) *(M L1)* ⭐ **In fact, this is not the northernmost point but still an unforgettable experience. The 307 m/1,017 ft high plateau on the island of Magerøy is 2,163 km/1,350 miles from Oslo.**

You reach the island through a 6.8 km/4¼ miles long tunnel and 45 minutes later you will arrive at the North Cape. There are restaurants, souvenirs, a panorama bar and a small ecumenical chapel in the gigantic *North Cape Hall.* But the real drama at latitude 71°10′21″ north is performed on the northern horizon from May to July if no fog or cloud veils the midnight sun. In summer, you won't find yourself alone here even in the middle of the night.

## SIGHTSEEING

### INSIDER TIP GJESVÆRSTAPPAN

You should try to get a close-up view of the spectacle taking place on this bird rock: cormorants, puffins, sea-gulls and sea eagles. Tours offered by *Gjesvær Turistsenter (in summer, three tours daily | 675 NOK per person | tel. 41 61 39 83 | www.birdsafari.com) and Roald Berg (daily | 500 NOK per person | Gjesvær | tel. 95 03 77 22 | www. stappan.no)*

### KIRKEPORTEN ＊

The hike to the "church door" rock is not very strenuous. From here, you have a fabulous view over the Norwegian Sea and towards the North Cape. *Starting point: near Kirkeporten Camping in Skarsvåg (see "Where to Stay")*

## WHERE TO STAY

### INSIDER TIP ARRAN NORDKAPP ＊

The loveliest place to stay on the island with fresh baked goods for breakfast. *40 rooms | Kamøyvær | tel. 75 40 20 85 | www. arran.as | Moderate*

### KIRKEPORTEN CAMPING

This camp site in the northern-most fishing village in the world also has well-insulated cabins and a lake at the door where the charr are just waiting to be hooked. *Skarsvåg | tel. 90 96 06 48 | www. kirkeporten.no | Budget*

## INFORMATION

*Turistinformasjon (Fiskeriveien 4 | Honningsvåg | tel. 78 47 70 30 | www. nordkapp.no)*

Almost the end of the world: where sky and sea meet at the North Cape

# VARANGER

(143 E–F 1–2) (*M–N 1–2*) **There are no trees and no green, only a lot of rocks and boulders on the ⭐ Varanger Peninsula.** *Tana Bru* is the hub of East Finnmark. This is where you cross the River Tana that has an exceptional reputation among salmon

In memory of a darker age: witch hunt memorial in Varanger

anglers. Road 89 leads to the Barents Sea and *Berlevåg* (135 km/84 miles) and *Båtsfjord* (108 km/67 miles). Stay on the 890 – the last 33 km/21 miles, the *Arctic Ocean Road*, between Kongsfjord and Berlevåg are a dream come true: storms, ice and saltwater have eroded the rocks and you will see sandy terraces between them.

*Vadsø* (pop. 6,200; 66 km/42 miles from Tana Bru) and *Vardø* (pop. 2,100; 141 km/85 miles) are melting pots of many cultures. In the 18th and 19th centuries, the Kven people came from Finland and sought

their luck as farmers, fishermen and miners. Russian factory ships lie at anchor in the harbour at Vardø – symbols of centuries of trade between Norway and Russia.

## WHERE TO GO

### INSIDER TIP HAMNINGBERG

This fishing village, which was spared from the ravages of the Second World War, is only inhabited in summer. The drive is worth it: 35 km/22 miles from Vardø with a moonlike landscape on the left-hand side and the Arctic Ocean on the right. You will be able to make out traces of movements in the earth's crust above the many beautiful beaches.

### STEILNESET MINNESTED (WITCHES' MEMORIAL) ●

Art on the Arctic Ocean: On a strip of land at the edge of Vardø, a you can walk through a 100 m/328 ft-long memorial designed by the Swiss architect Peter Zumthor and visit the mini museum with the *Burning Chair* by the French-American sculptor Louise Bourgeois that commemorate the witch hunts of the 17th century. *Freely accessible | free admission | www. nasjonaleturistveger.no*

### VADSØ MUSEUM (ESBENSGÅRDEN)

Here the culture of the Finnish-Norwegians (the Kvens) is fostered and passed on. The collections are displayed in a patrician house built in 1850 and a typical Kvene estate. *Mid-June–mid-Aug Tue–Sun 11am–5pm | admission 80 NOK | Hvistendahlgate 31 | www.varangermuseum.no*

### VARDØHUS FESTNING

Defence complex in Vardø built between 1734 and 1738, guarded by a commander and four soldiers, but now it is only an open-air museum. *Daily noon–5pm | admission 50 NOK | Festningsgaten 20*

## FOOD & DRINK

**HAVHESTEN RESTAURANT**
Reindeer meat? Kamchatka crabs? They taste best directly on the sea when it is sunny on the peninsula of Ekkerøy, 15 km/9 miles east of Vadsø. *Late June–mid-Aug / tel. 90 50 60 80 / www.ekkeroy.no / Moderate*

## WHERE TO STAY

**EKKERØY FERIEHUS**
Encounters with the world of Arctic nature on northern Norway's most famous bird "island" Ekkerøy with a wonderful view of Varangerfjord from these ecologically friendly holiday homes (with sauna). *3 houses / tel. 78 94 00 10 / www.ekkeroy.net / Budget–Moderate*

INSIDER TIP **KONGSFJORD GJESTEHUS**
Simply marvellous! With the Arctic Ocean at your feet, the simple but cosy rooms are a dream accommodation for all those who want to enjoy the nature of the Arctic with all their senses in a peaceful setting. The dishes conjured up by the innkeeper Åse – featuring fresh seafood delicacies – are also a delight. *18 rooms / Kongsfjord / Veines / tel. 78 98 10 00 / www.kongsfjord-gjestehus.no / Moderate*

## INFORMATION

*Båtsfjord: (Hindberggata 19 / tel. 78 98 34 00 / baatsfjord.kommune.no; Berlevåg Pensjonat & Camping AS / tel. 78 98 16 10 / www.berlevag-pensjonat.no; Tana: (Tana rådhus / tel. 46 40 02 00 / www.tana.kommune.no; Vadsø: Touristinformasjon (Kirkegata 1 / tel. 78 94 04 44 / www.varanger.com); Vardø: Touristinformasjon (Sentrum / tel. 78 98 69 07 / www.varanger.com)*

## WHERE TO GO

INSIDER TIP **SØR-VARANGER/ PASVIKTAL** (143 E–F 3–4) (*M–N3*)
After a long trip to the east, the E6 ends in *Kirkenes* (pop. 3,300). Here, the *Varanger Museum (www.varangermuseum.no)* shows how the region was affected by World War II. The western edge of the Siberian Taiga called *Pasvik valley*, now a national park, lies to the south of the town. A dense primeval forest with a great variety of flora makes for good hiking, but you should be careful – this is brown bear country. 40 km/25 miles further south, you can look over to the chimneys in Nikel in Russia from *Høyde 96 (Height 96)*. The *Skogfoss Waterfall* is only 50 m/164 ft from the Russian border. In the south of the national park, a heap of stones shows where Russia, Finland and Norway meet (5 km/3 miles from the end of the road in *Noatun*). *Information: Turistinformasjon Kirkenes (Dr. Wesselsgate 16 / tel. 46 51 24 20 / www.visitkirkenes.no)*

## LOW BUDGET

The pass for the *Nordkapp Film Festival (mid-September in Honningsvåg / www.nordkappfilmfestival.no)* only costs 550 NOK – a real bargain in expensive Norway!

With *Widerøe (www.wideroe.no)*, the most punctual regional airline in the world, you can get to every corner of northern Norway – it services 13 airports north of Tromsø. Every flight is an adventure, and the round trip ticket without restrictions costs just 340 euros in summer.

# DISCOVERY TOURS

## ① NORWAY AT A GLANCE

**START:** ① Oslo
**END:** ① Oslo

**Distance:**
🚗 3,700 km/2,300 miles

**11 days**
Driving time
(without stops)
65 hours

**COSTS:** 10,500 NOK (petrol, tolls, ferries, Hurtigruten with cabin, and a train ride with sleeping compartment)
**WHAT TO PACK:** hiking gear (hiking boots, rain gear, sun protection and a small backpack)

**IMPORTANT TIPS:**
The driving time specified refers to the distances travelled by car, Hurtigruten and train. Plan on an average speed (car) of 60 km/h at most in western Norway.
Train Bodø–Trondheim: book a sleeping compartment!

Would you like to explore the places that are unique to this country? Then the Discovery Tours are just the thing for you – they include terrific tips for stops worth making, breathtaking places to visit, selected restaurants and fun activities. It's even easier with the Touring App: download the tour with map and route to your smartphone using the QR Code on pages 2/3 or from the website address in the footer below – and you'll never get lost again even when you're offline.

TOURING APP

→ p. 2/3

On this round trip route departing from Oslo you can experience all the diversity of the Norwegian countryside from the Hardangervidda plateau and gigantic fjords to the coast brimming with offshore islands whose great beauty can only be truly appreciated from the water. Cross through endless forests and the broad valleys of eastern Norway on your way back to the capital.

The tour begins in ❶ Oslo → p. 41 with the view from the Holmenkollen ski jump – the perfect way to set the mood for this country of mountains, forests and fjords – and a stroll on the roof of the Opera House with a view of the Oslofjord behind you and ultra modern high rises in front.

| DAY 1 | |
|---|---|
| ❶ Oslo | ☀ 🏛 |

Photo: A stroll on the roof of the Opera House in Oslo

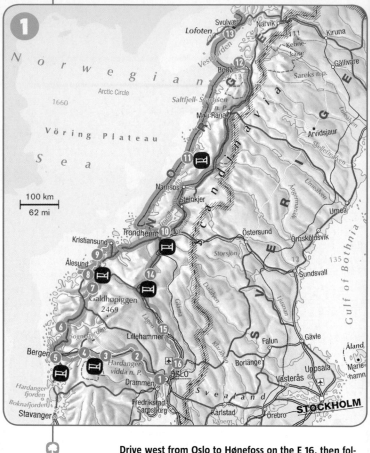

**1**

Svolvær
Lofoten
Narvik
411
Kiruna
Kebne-
kaise
Gällivare
Bodø
Sareks n.p.
Arctic Circle
Saltfjell- Svartisen
n. p.
Arvidsjaur
Mo i Rana
Vöring Plateau
Namsos
Steinkjer
Umeå
100 km
62 mi
Trondheim
Östersund
Örnsköldsvik
Kristiansund
Storsjön
Sundsvall
Ålesund
Galdhøpiggen
2469
Lillehammer
Falun
Gävle
Bergen
Åland
Mariehamn
Hardanger-
fjorden
Hardanger-
vidda n. P.
Drammen
OSLO
Borlänge
Uppsala
Västerås
Boknafjorden
Stavanger
Fredrikstad
Sarpsborg
Karlstad
Örebro
Svealand
**STOCKHOLM**

---

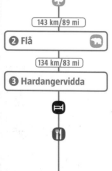

143 km / 89 mi

**② Flå**

134 km / 83 mi

**③ Hardangervidda**

**Drive west from Oslo to Hønefoss on the E 16,** then follow **Road 7** through forests and past lakes into the countryside. In **②** **Flå,** you can explore **Bjørneparken** *(early April–Oct daily 10am–4pm | admission 15 June–20 Aug 349 NOK, otherwise 299 NOK | bjorneparken.no).* Watch bears, moose and many other animals in a natural compound. Then you'll climb uphill to the **③** **Hardangervidda → p. 58.** At the edge of town, check into the mountain inn **INSIDER TIP** **Fagerheim Fjellstugu** *(20 rooms | Haugastøl | tel. 92 25 84 98 | www.fjellandfjord.com | Expensive)* for two nights. Enjoy the huge hiking area, the hearty fare and the innkeepers who know every corner of this Arctic wilderness like the back of their hands.

# DISCOVERY TOURS

Put on your hiking boots and spend the next day exploring the wide expanse of nature right before your doorstep!

**Continue along Road 7.** The fjords of Norway will come into view as you approach the small town of Eidfjord – the road winds between the steep rocky overhangs and the deep inlet towards the coast. The ❸ **Hardanger** → p. 57 region is home to the majority of Norway's orchards. Make sure to stop at ❹ **Hardangerfjord** → p. 57 and try some of the freshly-picked berries that are sold everywhere. Afterwards, ❺ **Bergen** → p. 52 awaits. Take in the fabulous view from the highest point on the **Fløibanen** in the middle of town.

Then **drive north on the E 39** and cross the huge ❻ **Sognefjord** → p. 60 by ferry. In **Byrkjelo, follow Road 60** along the Innvikfjorden, an arm of the Nordfjord → p. 61. The Norwegian Sea cuts deeply into the countryside, making for unforgettable experiences such as the **ferry ride from Hellesylt through** ❼ **Geirangerfjord** → p. 51 and a night's stay at **Petrines Gjestgiveri** → p. 52 **(Road 63).**

Keep heading north on **Road 63 to make the crossing with the Eidsdal–Linge ferry.** Once you've landed, follow **Road 650 along Norddalsfjord and past Stordal. In Sjøholt, take the E 39 westward to** ❽ **Ålesund** → p. 48. After a stroll through the art nouveau town, **return to the E 39.** Shortly past Molde → p. 59, turn off onto the ❾ **Atlantic Ocean Route** → p. 60 **(Road 664)** where you can almost cast a fishing line through the car window.

Norway's fjord landscape ends to the east of Kristiansund. Drive south through the underwater tunnel **from Kristiansund back to the E 39.** The forests close in as you head toward the interior of Norway until a fjord once again appears shortly before you come to ❿ **Trondheim** → p. 67. Park your car at the main railway station in this cathedral city. A stroll through the pleasant **Bakklandet** district on the eastern shore of the River Nidelva with its cafés and pubs is the perfect end to the day's travels.

**An adventure begins the next day aboard the** ⑪ **Hurtigruten** → p. 24. The ship glides north through the magical coastal landscape of Helgeland.c

The ship crosses the Arctic Circle and docks in ⑫ **Bodø** → p. 71 after 16 hours.

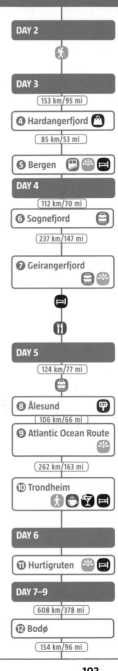

DAY 2

DAY 3
153 km/95 mi
④ Hardangerfjord
85 km/53 mi
⑤ Bergen

DAY 4
112 km/70 mi
⑥ Sognefjord
237 km/147 mi

⑦ Geirangerfjord

DAY 5
124 km/77 mi

⑧ Ålesund
106 km/66 mi
⑨ Atlantic Ocean Route
262 km/163 mi
⑩ Trondheim

DAY 6
⑪ Hurtigruten

DAY 7–9
608 km/378 mi
⑫ Bodø
154 km/96 mi

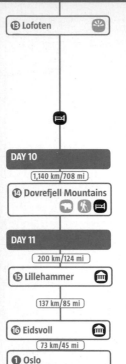

**⑬ Lofoten**

Bodø is the gateway to the **⑬ Lofoten → p. 80**. Stay on board after crossing the Vestfjord to travel through the enchanting **Trollfjord → p. 84** before the ship turns back in the harbour town of Stokmarknes. Although it is just past midnight, it is still light as day. In the afternoon, you'll head south, back to the Trollfjord and then Bodø, where night once again turns into day. Sit back and relax on the **train ride from Bodø to Trondheim**, and spend another night in Trondheim.

**DAY 10**

1,140 km/708 mi

**⑭ Dovrefjell Mountains**

**Drive south on the E 06.** Europe's largest population of musk oxen inhabits the **⑭ Dovrefjell Mountains → p. 64**. Take part in one of the guided hikes offered at **Hjerkinnhus Vandrerhjem** *(20 rooms | Dovrefjell | tel. 46 42 01 02 | www. hjerkinnhus.no | Budget)*.

**DAY 11**

200 km/124 mi

**⑮ Lillehammer**

**To the south of Dombås, the countryside around Gudbrandsdalen valley** opens up to the Olympic town of **⑮ Lillehammer → p. 39**. Check out the winter sport arenas and the open-air museum **Maihaugen** – once more a truly authentic taste of Norway.

137 km/85 mi

**⑯ Eidsvoll**

73 km/45 mi

**❶ Oslo**

On the way back to the capital, stop briefly in **⑯ Eidsvoll** and admire the impressively restored building in which the Norwegian constitution was ratified on 17 May 1814. Return to **❶ Oslo → p. 41**, the first and last stop on this route.

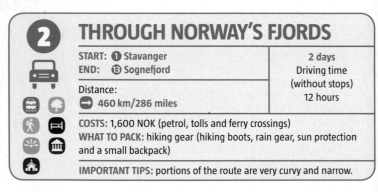

# ② THROUGH NORWAY'S FJORDS

| START: ❶ Stavanger | 2 days |
| END: ⑬ Sognefjord | Driving time |
| | (without stops) |
| Distance: | 12 hours |
| 🔵 460 km/286 miles | |

**COSTS:** 1,600 NOK (petrol, tolls and ferry crossings)
**WHAT TO PACK:** hiking gear (hiking boots, rain gear, sun protection and a small backpack)

**IMPORTANT TIPS:** portions of the route are very curvy and narrow.

Encounter the force of the water that has brought industry to the towns on the inner side of the fjord on the way to Stavanger up in the peaceful world of the mountain. Steer towards the two most beautiful fjords in western Norway, Hardangerfjord and Sognefjord, and the surrounding mountains. The three ferries on this route depart frequently so you won't have to wait long.

Start off in ❶ **Stavanger** → **p. 62**. First drive south **to Sandnes and follow Road 13 to the Lauvvik–Oanes ferry.** From the other side, **turn right shortly before Jørpeland to get to Preikestolshytta,** the starting point of the two-hour, sometimes challenging hike to the precipice ❷ **Preikestolen** → **p. 63**. The view of Lysefjord is most beautiful early in the morning.

Continue driving **on Road 13.** Ryfylke is an area full of valleys and forests, narrow fjords with lots of branches and the mountains that extend to the Setesdal in southern Norway. Put in a stop at ❸ **Årdal**. The view over the valley and the village from the **old church** (daily 9am–7pm), a gem from the early 17th century, is fantastic. After **crossing the Jøsenfjord by ferry,** enjoy the lovely view stretching for a few kilometres eastward down the fjord from Hjelmeland. Then, after a short bit of climbing, the route **continues to the narrow Erfjord and then to Sandsfjord.**

**Stay on Road 13 as it heads into the mountains.** The stretch along the lake Suldalsvatnet takes you away from the fjords for a while. At Breifonn, you will come to the **E 134** that leads to Hardanger → p. 57. The southern landmark of this holiday region with a rich tradition is the tumbling waterfall ❹ **Låtefossen**, which crashes into a river next to the road. **Drive further to the north,** and before long you will come to the ❺ **Odda Hytte & Gjestegård** (7 rooms, 1 cabin | Jordalsvegen 11B | Odda | tel. 99 27 23 63 | www.oddahytte.com | Budget) where you can spend a relaxing night.

In ❻ **Tyssedal,** tour the INSIDER TIP **Norwegian Museum of Hydro Power and Industry** (early June–early Sept daily 10am–5pm | admission 50 NOK | www.nvim.no). The power plant is an impressive construction dating to the period between 1900 and 1920 when hydro power became the pillar supporting Norway's energy supply and industrial development.

**DAY 1**

❶ **Stavanger**

65 km/40 mi

❷ **Preikestolen**

50 km/31 mi

❸ **Årdal**

153 km/95 mi

❹ **Låtefossen**

13 km/8 mi

❺ **Odda Hytte & Gjestegård**

**DAY 2**

8 km/5 mi

❻ **Tyssedal**

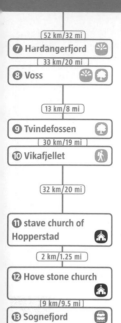

| 52 km/32 mi |
| **7** Hardangerfjord |
| 33 km/20 mi |
| **8** Voss |

| 13 km/8 mi |
| **9** Tvindefossen |
| 30 km/19 mi |
| **10** Vikafjellet |

| 32 km/20 mi |

| **11** stave church of Hopperstad |
| 2 km/1.25 mi |
| **12** Hove stone church |
| 9 km/9.5 mi |
| **13** Sognefjord |

After crossing the gigantic, 1,300 m (4,265 ft) long **hanging bridge over 7 Hardangerfjord → p. 57**, it is not far to **8 Voss**. This winter sports town is a paradise for extreme sport enthusiasts. The meadows on the banks of the Vangsvannet lake in the middle of town are a great place to stop and take a break.

Soon after you pass by the rushing waters of **9 Tvindefossen**, the route begins **to climb to the pass of 10 Vikafjellet**. Once you reach the top, stop at the rest area on the southern part of the pass and head off into the mountains for a few hours.

Return to the car, **and turn left shortly before Vik** to the **11 stave church of Hopperstad (Hopperstad Stavkirke)** *(daily 10am–5pm | admission 70 NOK),* constructed around 1150, whose Gothic altar baldachin is decorated with impressive carvings. On the other side of the street, you will see the small **12 Hove stone church** (2nd half of the 12th century), the oldest building in the region. This is the last stop before **13 Sognefjord → p. 60**, which you will **now follow for a few minutes to Vangsnes** where the ferries depart for Hella.

The Tvindefossen cascades into the valley near the town of Voss

# NORWAY'S DREAM COAST

| START: ❶ Steinkjer<br>END: ⓮ Bodø | 5 days<br>Driving time<br>(without stops)<br>20 hours |
| --- | --- |
| Distance:<br>➡ 940 km/584 miles | |

**COSTS:** 2,100 NOK (petrol and ferries)

**IMPORTANT TIPS:** more information about Road 17 is available from *Kystriksveien (www.kystriksveien.no).*

Norway's longest and most beautiful detour is Road 17, known as the "slow way to the north". Sandy beaches and waterfalls, the blue sea and sun-drenched mountains, islands, powerful glaciers and the light of the Nordland – you will need plenty of time to explore this stretch of coast between Trondheim and Bodø. You will have to wait an hour at the most for the next ferry.

**Drive northwards from ❶ Steinkjer to the Holm–Vennesund ferry.** You can seen the Torghatten mountain in the distance from the pier in ❷ **Vennesund**. It has a unique feature, namely a hole that the sea eroded out of the rock. Stay in Vennesund and enjoy the sunset on Nordland's coast. You can find a place to sleep at **Vennesund Brygge og Camping** *(3 rorbus, 14 cabins | tel. 75 02 73 75 | www.vennesund.no | Budget).*

**The destinations for the next day are ❸ Brønnøysund** and **Torghatten**, which you've already admired from afar. The mountain lies 15 km/9 miles to the west on an island. A 20-minute walk will bring you to the hole that is 160 m/525 ft wide and 35 m/115 ft high – plus a marvellous view and fresh sea air.

**8 km/5 miles north of Brønnøysund,** Tilrem is home to the herb garden ❹ **Hildurs Urterarium** *(June–Aug daily 10am– 5pm | admission 50 NOK | www.hildurs.no).* Although the Arctic Circle is close by, the herb soup is made with ingredients from the garden. After a twenty-minute crossing on the **Horn–Anndalsvågen ferry and a lovely 17 km/10.5 miles stretch along the coast**, you will come to ❺ **Vevelstad** and ❻ **Forvik**. At the ferry terminal, you will find the 200 year-old trading post INSIDER TIP **Forvikgården,**

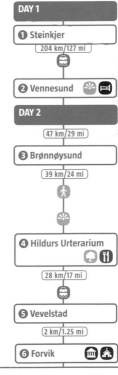

**DAY 1**

❶ Steinkjer

204 km/127 mi

❷ Vennesund

**DAY 2**

47 km/29 mi

❸ Brønnøysund

39 km/24 mi

❹ Hildurs Urterarium

28 km/17 mi

❺ Vevelstad

2 km/1.25 mi

❻ Forvik

A painted door on the old rectory in Alstahaug

and the **local museum** and **church** (1796) with an altar-piece by Joseph Pisani a bit further on.

**The next ferry needs an hour to sail to Tjøtta. Drive 19 km/11 miles further to ⑦ Alstahaug**, the heart of Nordland. Looking inward, you will see the Seven Sisters Mountains. Next to the 12th century church and almost on the banks of the lake, take a look at the the residence of the priest and poet Petter Dass (1647–1707) and the nearby **Petter Dass Museum** *(mid-June–mid-Aug daily 10am–6pm, otherwise shorter hours | admission 100 NOK | www.petter-dass.no)*. The landmark of the fishing town of ⑧ **Sandnessjøen** (pop. 5,300) is a 1,000 m/3,280 ft long hanging bridge. Plan to spend two nights in **Rica Hotel Syv Søstre** *(69 rooms | Torolv Kveldulvsonsgate 16 | tel. 75 06 50 00 | www.rica.no | Moderate)* to explore the islands of Nordland.

Travel with the regular **liner to the enchanting islands of** ⑨ **Lovund → p. 77** and ⑩ **Træna → p. 77** – a day trip out

🚆

(35 km/22 mi)

⑦ Alstahaug 🏛

(21 km/13 mi)

⑧ Sandnessjøen 🛏

**DAY 3**

(52 km/32 mi)

⑨ Lovund 🎁

(25 km/15.5 mi)

⑩ Træna 🎁

on the sea to visit the hospitable inhabitants who still live from fishing and the rocks with huge colonies of seabirds.

**The Levang–Nesna ferry runs north of Sandnessjøen.** The mountains now come closer on land. The one-hour **ferry crossing Kilboghamn–Jektvik** is quite special thanks to the imaginary Arctic Circle. The **Ågskaret–Forøy ferry** waits just 28 km/17.4 miles beyond Jektvik. The **Engabreen**, a glacier snout of the **Svartisen → p. 76**, has shifted almost to the open sea within the ⑪ **Holandsfjord**. You can get close to the wrinkled mass of ice with one of the boat tours leaving from Holand or Braset. Spend the night at the mouth of the fjord with a view of the Norwegian Sea at **Furøy Camping** *(20 cabins/ Halsa / tel. 94 19 13 15 / www.furoycamp.no | Budget).*

After **crossing through the Svartisen tunnel**, you will come to the industrial town of Glomfjord and then Ørnes. 38 km/23.6 miles to the north, take a **detour on Road 838 to ⑫ Gildeskål** and walk through the little town to the **church** *(guided tours in summer)* built before 1250. Enjoy the peace, the idyllic harbour and the fantastic view in all directions.

**Return to Road 17** and drive on to the turbulent waters of the ⑬ **Saltstraumen → p. 76**. Road 17 ends just a few kilometres beyond this maelstrom best viewed from above. **In Løding, turn onto Road 80** to ⑭ **Bodø → p. 71**, the end of this route.

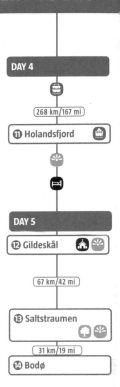

**DAY 4**

268 km/167 mi

⑪ Holandsfjord

**DAY 5**

⑫ Gildeskål

67 km/42 mi

⑬ Saltstraumen

31 km/19 mi

⑭ Bodø

---

# 4 FROM THE CAPITAL CITY TO THE WORLD HERITAGE SITE

| START: ❶ Oslo | 2 days |
| END: ❽ Bergen | Travelling time (without stops) 13 hours |
| Distance: ➡ 530 km/329 miles (incl. 82 km/51 miles cycling) | |

**COSTS:** 1,670 NOK (train tickets and bicycle rental)
**WHAT TO PACK:** weatherproof clothing, cycling gear (helmet!)

**IMPORTANT TIPS:**
The cycling route is only viable from mid-July to early September because of snowfall and there are some very steep inclines.
❼ **Flåms Railway:** departs approx. every two hours in summer. Info on travel and booking options available from *Fjord Tours (www. fjordtours.com)* and the Norwegian state railway *(www.nsb.no).*

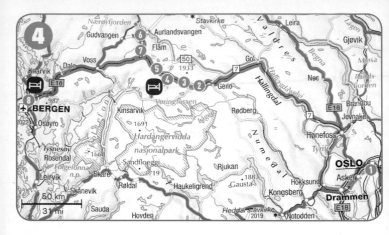

On the trip from Oslo into the land of the fjords, you will find alpine landscapes with good cycling paths but no roads. After heading up with the train, you will tackle two stretches by bike to the edge of the Hardangerjøkulen glacier. The famous Flåms railway and the Bergen train will then bring you to Bergen.

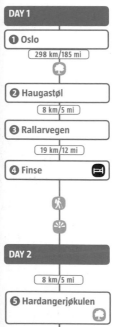

**DAY 1**

**❶ Oslo**

298 km/185 mi

**❷ Haugastøl**

8 km/5 mi

**❸ Rallarvegen**

19 km/12 mi

**❹ Finse**

**DAY 2**

8 km/5 mi

**❺ Hardangerjøkulen**

The train departs  ❶ **Oslo** → p. 41 **in the morning from the main station,** carrying you past the cities of Drammen and Hønefoss to the forested valley of Hallingdal. Then it's all uphill from there – **to the railway station at ❷ Haugastøl,** which sits about 300 km/186 miles away from Oslofjord and 988 m/3,241 ft higher. Pick up your rental bikes and tackle the first stretch of the ❸ **Rallarvegen** → p. 113.

On the first part of the route on the old construction road along the Bergen railway tracks, you will find a good path (not paved with asphalt) **from Haugastøl to ❹ Finse:** the "roof of Norway" at a height of 1,222 m/4,009 ft. Stay for a night at the **Finse Hotel** *(43 rooms | tel. 56 52 71 00 | www.finse1222.no | full board only | Expensive)* and take an evening stroll along the lake or enjoy the terrace with its glacier view.

The **second stretch of the cycling tour** may head downhill, but it is no less challenging. Even in summer, you can come upon snowdrifts and the weather up here is quite temperamental. The ❺ **Hardangerjøkulen** glacier watches over travellers who need to be quite careful on some of the curves, especially **after passing the Hotel Vatnahalsen where the sometimes steep decline into the val-**

**ley of Flamsdålen** begins. You will have to stay focused on the last 10 km/6 miles because you will descend a height of about 800 m/2,625 ft as the mighty rock walls block the wind.

**You will arrive at the Aurlandsfjord in ⑥ Flåm,** which is a Unesco World Heritage Site. The hustle and bustle at the last station on the world-famous Flåm Railway is a real shock after the peace and quiet of the last two days. Turn in your rental bikes and have lunch at the `INSIDER TIP` **Ægir Bryggeri** *(www.flamsbrygga.no/aegir-bryggeri/ | Budget),* a successful microbrewery run by a New Yorker and a Norwegian. If you have time, stop by the **Flåmsbana Museum** *(www.visitflam.com)* in a former station building. Then it is time to pass through 20 tunnels and around several tight bends **with the ⑦ Flåm Railway → p. 61 back into the mountains.** Over a stretch of 20 km/12.4 miles, the electric-driven railway climbs a height of 865 m/2,838 ft.

**In Myrdal, switch over to the Bergen railway to head to the city of Bergen.** You will pass through the town of Voss and countless tunnels as well as other fjords on the approx. two-hour journey to **⑧ Bergen → p. 52.** Give your body and mind a rest after the day's many impressions at a fine hotel with good food near the train station, the **Grand Hotel Terminus** *(131 rooms | Zander Kaaesgate 6 | tel. 55 21 25 00 | www.grandterminus.no | Moderate).* Bergen is the last stop on this trip through southern Norway.

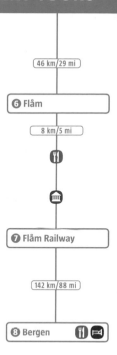

| 46 km/29 mi |
| ⑥ Flåm |
| 8 km/5 mi |
| 🍴 |
| 🏛 |
| ⑦ Flåm Railway |
| 142 km/88 mi |
| ⑧ Bergen 🍴🚆 |

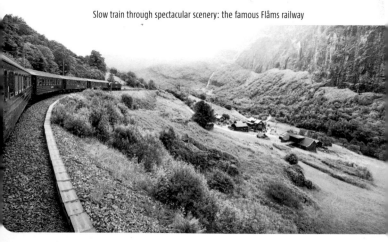

Slow train through spectacular scenery: the famous Flåms railway

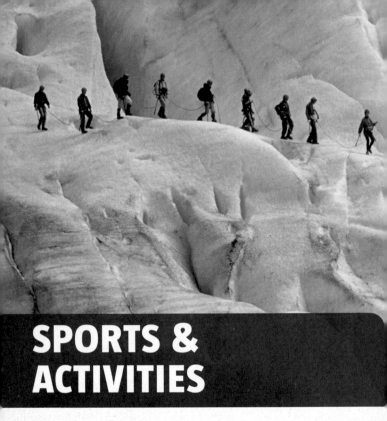

# SPORTS & ACTIVITIES

**Norway is becoming an increasingly popular destination for people seeking extreme challenges. But Norway also has a lot to offer to those holiday-makers who just want to be on the move.**

Coasts and fjords, fantastic rivers and lakes at all elevations are perfect for anglers and water sports enthusiasts, while the mountains offer challengers to hikers and mountaineers. And since Norway is home to the "cradle of skiing", winter sports naturally take centre stage.

## ANGLING

Norway is a paradise for anglers and especially those who love to trawl the coast for the best fishing spots. Every inhabited island and coastal town has areas that cater especially to fishing enthusiasts. Angling in the sea and fjord is free, but sport fishing in rivers and lakes requires permission from the leaseholder (contact the Tourist Information Office for more details). If you aim to catch salmon and sea trout, you need to pay a 260 NOK fee *(fiskeravgift)*. This can be done ahead of time on-line (fiskeravgift.miljodirektoratet.no). You should also pay attention to the export regulations (see p. 125).

## CYCLING

Explore Norway by bike: Bikes can be hired directly at the most popular cycling routes or at the airports *(Fly & Bike)*. An easier option is the electric bikes available in *Hammerfest (www.hammerfesttu*

**Norway's coasts, plateaus and mountains offer a great many possibilities for you to test your fitness**

*rist.no)* for guided tours. The challenging *Rallarvegen* between Oslo and Bergen takes cyclists through the wild and rugged Hardangervidda. The *Jæren* region which starts in *Stavanger* is more suitable for children. In *Andenes* at the northern tip of Vesterålen, a 450 km/280 mile long cycling route starts and runs to Å, the most southerly point of the Lofoten Islands. Off-road bikers can hire bikes and equipment from the *Hafjell Bikepark (www. hafjell.no)*. You can find descriptions of all the bike trails in Norway and order a practical guide from *www.cyclingnorway. com.*

## EXTREME SPORTS

Ice climbing in *Hemsedal*, rafting along the raging *Trysilelva* River, wreck diving in *Vestland*, ski-mountaineering over the *Hardangervidda* – the Norwegian landscape offers countless sporting activities in summer and winter which will push your body to its limits. Beginners can also try their luck and are assisted by experienced instructors who make sure the emphasis is on fun. More experienced athletes should take part in the ● *Birkebeiner (www.birkebeiner.no)* to test their abilities against like-minded adrenalin junkies. Whether you choose the cross-country skiing (54 km/34 miles), cycling (100 km/62 miles) and crosscountry running (21 km/13 miles) races - Norway's rugged nature and unpredictable weather will put your endurance and stamina to the test.

## GOLF

Only true golf addicts will take their clubs to Norway. The country offers the chance to play on some of the world's most unusual golf courses. *Meland* near Bergen is regarded as the most challenging of all. The world's most northerly course, the *Tromsø Golf Park,* also appeals to avid golfers. Probably the most beautiful of all is the nine-hole *Lofoten Golfbane (www.lofoten-golf.no)* located directly next to the open sea surrounded by cliffs. You can play on the green until late in the evening in summer under the light of the midnight sun. *Norges Golfforbund (tel. 21 02 91 50 | www.golfforbundet.no)*

## MOUNTAINEERING & HIKING

Space and seclusion can be found all over Norway. The well-marked trails and simple to comfortable cabins make the high plateaus, mountains and islands particularly attractive destinations. Backpackers are especially fond of the *Saltfellet-Svartisen* and *Øvre Pasvik* national parks in northern Norway, *Bjørgefjell* and *Dovrefjell-Sunndalsfjella* in the centre of the country, *Jotunheimen* and *Rondane* in the south – and, of course, the *Hardangervidda*. The cabins are usually located three to eight hours walk from each other. You can obtain detailed information from the Norwegian Hiking Association DNT *(Oslo | tel. 40 00 18 70 | www.turistforeningen.no)*. Almost all the *DNT* routes are described briefly at *www.ut.no*.

*DNT* also provides essential information for mountaineers, climbers & co. The most popular areas are the demanding peaks in the west of *Jotunheimen* and around *Jostedalsbreen* glacier. Glacier hikes with experienced guides are offered there, as well as at *Folgefonna glacier (tel. 95 11 77 92 | www.folgefonni-breforarlag.no)* near Hardangerfjord, throughout the summer. *Bergtatt Stryn (tel. 95 20 11 92 | www.norwegianmountains.no)* in the western region of Nordfjord is a very good address (for mountain bike tours as well). Local mountaineering clubs can be contacted through the tourist information offices.

## SKIING

In a country with so much space there must be a lot of cross-country trails. They begin in front of the house or cabin door, are often floodlit, and can run for dozens of kilometres. And, you can be sure of there being snow from November to April – at least east of the fjords and from Nordland to the North Cape.

Alpine skiers have also discovered Norway and they can choose from a handful of first-class destinations. *Trysilfjellet (www.skistar.com/trysil)* near the Swedish border is an ideal ski resort for families as is the Olympic town of *Lillehammer. Geilo (www.geilo.no)*, halfway between Oslo and Bergen, offers the best combination of alpine and cross-county skiing. Young alpinists who are into off-slope skiing travel to *Stranda (www.strandafjellet.no)* near Ålesund or Hemsedal *(www.hemsedal.com)*.

## SPAS

Sports activities may offer some enough of a break from everyday life, but Norway's spas are like the ice cream on the cake when it comes to relaxation. The *Solstrand Hotel & Bad (Os | tel. 56 57 11 00 | www.solstrand.com)* south of Bergen is a classic with spa treatments for body and face, massage baths, steam baths and a Finnish sauna as well as a swim in the Bjørnefjord. The *Hotel Alexandra (Loen | tel. 57 87 50 00 | www.alexandra.no)* on Nordfjord and the *Sola Strand Hotel (s. p. 63)* south of Stavanger have a similar offering. ● **INSIDER TIP** *The Well (Kongeveien 65 | Sofiemyr | tel. 48 04 48 88 | 20 minutes south of Oslo)* is stylish and offers a break from everyday life, where you can indulge in a full day of tranquillity, wellness and revitalisation. The choice ranges from a Japanese bathhouse, tropical sauna, hamam or waterfall grotto. Once you arrive, you'll never want to leave.

## WATER SPORTS

The entire south coast from Oslo to Egersund is a superb sailing area and it often gets quite crowded in the harbours. However, you will always find a calm bay where you can drop anchor. The harbours to the north are more sheltered and also have more room.

Canoes and kayaks are more Norwegian: offers range from tours along the coast and in the fjords to trips from lake to lake (with your tent and sturdy shoes in your kit) and white-water courses on one of the rivers that flow from the alpine regions to the east or west. The number one address for this is *Sjoa,* a tributary of the Lågen in the upper Gudbrandsdalen region. There are half, one or two-day tours. Information: *Sjoa Rafting (Heidal | tel. 90 07 10 00 | www.sjoarafting.com).* You will get a taste of the Arctic on a kayak tour on the **INSIDER TIP** *glacial lakes at Jostedalsbreen* offered by *Icetroll (Breheimsenteret Jostedal | tel. 97 01 43 70 | www.icetroll.com).*

Icy adventures: ocean canoe tours on the Jostedalsbreen glacier

# TRAVEL WITH KIDS

**At first glance, the long journey to get to Norway, the enormous distances in the country itself and the high prices might make you think that Norway is not really the place for a family holiday. Nevertheless, many parents set off for the north with their children on the back seat year after year.**

It is also not so difficult if you decide to use public transport: many trains have family compartments and open-plan carriages with play corners. These can also be found on all of the ferries to Norway, the major ferries on the fjords and Hurtigruten ships. Baby-care rooms and highchairs are taken for granted – even in most restaurants. There are children's menus and nobody minds children playing. Norway is a country that loves children.

Many families prefer to spend their holidays in a cabin. There are enough bedrooms, rustic furnishing and small playgrounds near the house are standard. Children want to enjoy themselves outdoors and there is plenty of that in Norway. Zoos and theme parks, aquariums, riding schools, farms, safe beaches in the interior and on the coast – or boundless sledging and skiing in the Norwegian winter – ensure that there will never be even a hint of boredom.

A trip to northern Norway does require a certain amount of planning. The enormous distances, the lack of urban attractions and the possibility of rainy weather can make the young ones a bit restless. Tip: park the car and travel part of the way with one of the Hurtigruten ships or take

**Holidays in summer or winter are a lot of fun: there is always something new waiting to be discovered in this country with so much space**

a catamaran to a fishing village on one of the islands. The hustle and bustle on the quay usually keeps children entertained.

## THE SOUTH

### BØ SØMMARLAND ⚓

(137 D4) (*ⓜ C17*)

Northern Europe's largest water fun park is located in the beautiful high hills of the Telemark region. Especially in summer, this is an ideal place to spend an entire day. The children can really let their hair down on the enormous water-mountain-and-valley run, as well as a gigantic half-pipe and artificial surfing wave. *Early June–mid-Aug daily 10am–7pm | admission, adults 289 NOK, children (3–4½ ft tall) 279 NOK, free under 95 cm; cheaper tickets online | Steintjønnvegen 2 | Bø i Telemark | www.sommarland.no*

### INSIDER TIP▶ EVENTYRFABRIKKEN

(137 E5) (*ⓜ D17*)

The largest covered playground in Norway is located close to the E6. It is a five-storey jungle of bouncy castles, trampolines, ladders, tunnels and many other games. There is also a café. *Daily 10am–8pm | admission: adults free, 159 NOK for children up to age 17 | Vestengveien 40 | Sarpsborg | www.eventyrfabrikken.no*

## HUNDERFOSSEN FAMILIEPARK
(137 D–E2) *(ΩΩ D15)*

This is where the world's biggest troll lives – he is 14 m/46 ft high (when sitting down) – there is also a fairy-tale castle and grotto, a wax museum, car tracks and a place for swimming. The energy centre provides informative entertainment and shows how electricity is produced using water power. *Mid-June–mid-Aug daily 10am–6pm, otherwise 10am–5pm | 410 NOK, children (90–120 cm) 355 NOK | in Fåberg, 13 km/8 miles north of Lillehammer on the E6 | www.hunderfossen.no*

## KRISTIANSAND DYREPARK
(136 C6) *(ΩΩ B18)*

Located 11 km/7 miles east of Kristiansand, this is the only real zoo in Norway and is home to around 800 animals and birds. You should also visit the people living in *Kardemomme By*: the children's book *When the Robbers came to Cardamom Town* by Thorbjørn Egner has become reality in this miniature town. *Early July–early Aug daily 10am–7pm, otherwise 10am–5pm | admission: adults 399 NOK, children (3–13 years) 339 NOK, cheaper online | www.dyreparken.no*

## MINERALPARKEN (136 C6) *(ΩΩ B18)*

There are lots more to see besides minerals and stones at this park. Children will have a great time making their own jewellery and figurines. The park also offers numerous activities including canoeing, climbing and more besides for the whole family to enjoy. *Late June–mid- Aug daily 10am–6pm | ad-*

*mission: adults 195 NOK, children (3–13 years) 170 NOK | Mineralvegen 1 | Hornes | on Road 9 | 56 km/35 miles northeast of Kristiansand | www.mineralparken.no*

## NATURHISTORISK MUSEUM
(137 E4) *(ΩΩ D16)*

The skeletons of prehistoric animals are really fascinating! The 47-million-year-old primate "Ida" has made the Oslo museum a real hit with the public. The *Botanical Garden* with its scented garden is the perfect place to take the children for a picnic on a warm summer day. *Museum daily 11am–4pm, garden daily 7am–9pm | admission museum: adults 80 NOK, children (6–16) 40 NOK, families 200 NOK | Sarsgate 1 | at the Munch Museum / www.nhm.uio.no*

## THE WEST

## ATLANTIKPARK ÅLESUND
(140 A5) *(ΩΩ B13)*

Several landscaped aquariums have been carefully imbedded in the maritime environment of Norway's most modern aquarium. The largest pool contains 4 million litres of water and is the home of all of the species of fish that live off the coast of western Norway. The daily highlight is when a diver goes underwater to feed the fish. *June–Aug Sun–Fri 10am–6pm, Sat until 4pm, otherwise Mon–Sat 11am–4pm, Sun until 6pm | admission: adults 180 NOK, children 80 NOK | Tueneset | Ålesund | www.atlanterhavsparken.no*

## VILVITE THEME CENTRE
(136 A3) *(ΩΩ A15)*

This interactive science centre is located in Bergen on the E39 to the south of the city. Here, children and youths will be able to immerse themselves in the world of natural science and technology. Among the many subjects dealt with are weather, energy and the ocean. With experiments, an underwater world, ship and oil rig simulators, a café and a shop. *Late June–mid-Aug daily 10am–5pm, otherwise Tue–Fri 9am–3pm, Sat/Sun 10am–5pm | admission: adults 175 NOK, children (3–15 years) 145 NOK | Thormøhlens gate 51 | www.vilvite.no*

## LOFOTEN

### LOFOTAKVARIET (140 B3) (*ⓜ F7*)

Mainly animals that live in the Norwegian Sea swim in the pools of the Lofoten Aquarium near Svolvær. Children are particularly fond of the sea otters and seals. *June–Aug daily 10am–6pm, otherwise Sun–Fri 11am–3pm | admission: adults 130 NOK, children 70 NOK, families 340 NOK | Kabelvåg | Storvågen district | www.lofotakvariet.no*

## TROMS

### POLARIA (142 A3) (*ⓜ G5*)

A fantastic information and adventure centre in Tromsø: in addition to the widescreen cinema with a film about the polar regions, there is an aquarium and a seal pool, as well as exhibitions on polar research. *In summer daily 10am–7pm, otherwise 10am–5pm | admission: adults 130 NOK, children 65 NOK | Hjalmar Johansensgate 12 | www.polaria.no*

### POLARPARK (141 D2) (*ⓜ G6*)

Norway's "National Predatory Animal Centre" lies around 70 km/44 miles north of Narvik in the Salangsdalen valley. The "polar" animal life includes the elk, musk oxen and reindeer as well as wolves, lynxes and brown bears. *June–Aug daily 10am–6pm | admission: adults 260 NOK, children (3–15 years) 160 NOK, families 750 NOK | Bardu (E6, signposted from Fossbakken) | www.polarpark.no*

Waving for the cameras: Feeding time at the Atlantikpark Ålesund

# FESTIVALS & EVENTS

## FESTIVALS & EVENTS

### JANUARY

*International Film Festival Tromsø (www. tiff.no):* The festival season starts in icy cold and complete darkness. You can see the northern lights and an excellent films are screened in the second week in January

### MARCH/APRIL

*Holmenkollen Ski Festival in Oslo (skifest. no):* As many as 50,000 spectators make the competition from the famous Holmenkollen jump a real carnival. Second weekend in March

INSIDER TIP *Vossajazz (www.vossajazz. no):* Anybody interested in experiencing the perfect synthesis between international folk music and jazz should visit Voss in western Norway on the weekend before Easter. No venue is too small for this world music event

★ *Easter Festival in Kautokeino and Karasjok (www.samieasterfestival.com):* The Sami festival week filled with weddings, christenings and other family festivities, concerts, theatre performances, snow-scooter and reindeer races

### MAY/JUNE

May 17 is ★ ● *Constitution Day* (National Holiday) in Norway, which is celebrated with colourful parades, lots of music and traditional costumes *(bunad)* of the different regions. The festivities in Oslo – including a procession of children to the palace – and Bergen are especially impressive. The decorations always include fresh birch twigs along with the national flag

*Bergen Festival (www.fib.no)* and *Nattjazz (www.nattjazz.no):* Bergen really lets its hair down for ten days from the end of May to the beginning of June. Top artists from all over the world, free concerts, and music in the streets

### JUNE

The *Hardanger Music Festival (www.har dangermusikfest.no)* with folk music, chamber and church music, is held on the first weekend in June in a landscape in which Edvard Grieg composed many of his best-known works

*Midsummer Night (Sankthans)* is celebrated throughout Norway on 23 June with bonfires and a great deal of alcohol, even if it falls mid-week

At the end of June, the *Risør Chamber Music Festival (www.kammermusikkfest.*

*no)* takes place. During these five days concerts are given by both up-and-coming performers and international stars. All of this set against the blue of the Skagerrak and the white houses of the small town; shrimps and white wine are served on the quay

### JULY

*Moldejazz* (*www.moldejazz.no*) is still the biggest and – in terms of the surroundings – most beautiful of all the Norwegian jazz festivals. This is where world-famous artists and club bands appear and there are concerts on street corners, in small bars and even on a stage in the open-air museum. In the third week in July in Molde

*Battle of Stiklestad* (*www.stiklestad.no*): Events that took place in 1030 when Olav lost his life fighting for the crown are revived in the 'Saint Olav's Play' performed in an open air museum near Verdal north of Trondheim. The evening performances have a special ambiance. Last week in July

### AUGUST

In the second week in August, treats for the ears and palate come together during the *Sildajazz Festival* (*www.sildajazz.no*)

in Haugesund in western Norway. There is jazz on the streets and in the pubs, and a great variety of herrings at the harbour The *Øyafestival* (*www.oyafestival.com*) in Tøyenpark near the Munch Museum in Oslo has developed into the best open-air rock festival in Norway. On the second weekend in August

## NATIONAL HOLIDAYS

| | |
|---|---|
| 1 Jan | New Year's Day |
| 18 April 2019, 9 April 2020 | |
| | Holy Thursday |
| 19 April 2019, 10 April 2020 | |
| | Good Friday |
| 22 April 2019, 13 April 2020 | |
| | Easter Monday |
| 1 May | Labour Day |
| 17 May | Constitution Day (National Holiday) |
| 30 May 2019, 21 May 2020 | |
| | Ascension |
| 10 June 2019, 1 June 2020 | |
| | Whit Monday |
| 25/26 Dec | Christmas (celebrations start in the afternoon of the 24th) |

# LINKS, BLOGS, APPS & MORE

www.visitnorway.com Official website of the Norwegian Tourist Board (Innovation Norway). Comprehensive information about nature, destinations, cities, accommodation, holidays, camping and all the places you plan to visit – and others you will have on your list for your next trip

www.norway.org.uk Norway's official website in the UK which has information on planning a trip to Norway, embassy and consulate details, studying or working there as well as facts and figures about the country, its culture and history (www.norway.org for the USA site)

www.fjordnorway.com This tourism website specializes in the fjord area with tips for things to do and places to go as well as planning your trip and even booking accommodation or tours. Videos and panoramic photos will give you a taste of Norway from afar

www.tnp.no This is the website of Norway's English language newspaper in *The Nordic Page*. It caters to the international community and has local and international news as well as sections for art, culture, health and a multimedia section with videos and photographs. You can also follow their updates via Facebook and Twitter

Norgesbooking.com Have you ever wanted to try the authentic Norwegian cabin experience? This online site offers a wide choice of private cabins to be rented at the seaside and in the mountains

www.travbuddy.com/Norway-travel-guide-c215 This is a perfect internet address for anybody who is looking for somebody to travel with and also helps find friendly Norwegians who want to make interested people from abroad aware of all their country has to offer. You will find guides and tips to more than 650 individual destinations including many out-of-the-way places most tourists do not visit

Whether you are still researching your trip or are already in Norway, you will find more valuable information, videos and networks to add to your holiday experience at these links

www.newsinenglish.no View and News from Norway is a blog and news site set up by the Californian ex-editor of the Norwegian *Aftenposten* after it stopped its English language service. The site reports on issues of interest to the expat community and it also has a rather quirky link to Moose News which features moose-related articles

www.ninside.org Norway International Network is a 'dynamic and inclusive association with the goal of building a social and professional network'. Networking opportunities are provided through their meetings, online forums and discussion groups. The network also organises social activities

vimeo.com/2269307 Wonderfully poetic time-lapse recordings of picture-perfect Norwegian skies. As one of the comments aptly notes, "If nature were a book this film-maker would be a poet"

www.youtube.com/watch?v=Vd09-1HaOxg Although this clip of an extensive tour through the regions of southern and central Norway dates from the year 2009, it is guaranteed to bring back memories for those who have visited the area themselves and make those who have not think about where to spend their next holidays

www.youtube.com/watch?v=15UPi6rkfzO&list=PLHQjOOeWAFeILekMxgXGXxES qvadl74Yh&index=29 Informative video documenting a fishing trip in northern Norway with lots of practical information, a local skipper and pretty landscapes

**VIDEOS & MUSIC**

Navmii GPS Norway HD Navigation software for your iPad to make sure that you don't lose your way on any of the roads between the Skagerrak and Arctic Circle

NorCamp – camping in Norway Lots of information on the camp sites in your region. Comments and reviews help visitors choose the right site

Visitnorway.com – nearby – use the free app for iPhone and Android to find accommodation, activities, events, restaurants and place to go

**APPS**

# TRAVEL TIPS

## ARRIVAL

✈ A number of different airlines offer regular flights from the UK to Norway, some of which are surprisingly cheap. British Ariways (www.britishairways.com) and SAS (www.flysas.com), as well as the no-frills airlines Norwegian Air Shuttle (www.norwegian.com) and Ryanair (www.ryanair.com), among others, fly out of various British airports to Oslo, Bergen, Haugesund, Stavanger and Trondheim. It is worth noting that "Oslo" Torp is around 80 miles from central Oslo; the main Gardemoen International airport is much closer and benefits from a fast train service.

There are also a number flights to Norway from Scotland, in particular from Aberdeen, which service the oil industry.

## RESPONSIBLE TRAVEL

It doesn't take a lot to be environmentally friendly whilst travelling. Don't just think about your carbon footprint whilst flying to and from your holiday destination but also about how you can protect nature and culture abroad. As a tourist it is especially important to respect nature, look out for local products, cycle instead of driving, save water and much more. If you would like to find out more about eco-tourism please visit: www.ecotourism.org

Flights to and from the US and Canada go via Copenhagen, Stockholm or other European airports.

🚢 The last car ferry route between the UK and Norway (Newcastle to Bergen) was withdrawn in September 2008. However several ferries operate between Norway and mainland Europe (e.g. to Denmark; www.norwaydirect.com). Most operators offer package deals for a car and passengers, and most lines offer concessions. An additional charge is normally made for bicycles and boats.

🚆 Travelling from London to Norway by train is possible but takes a long time. If you take a lunchtime Eurostar to Brussels, a connecting high-speed train to Cologne, the overnight train to Copenhagen and connecting trains to Oslo, you arrive in the evening the day after leaving London.

An InterRail Pass can be recommended for a trip to Scandinavia (www.interrailnet.com). The InterRail Norway Pass is available for 3, 4, 6 or 8 "flexi" days within one month and costs from £170 (25% discount for those under 28). With the pass you can use some bus and ferry lines free of charge and there are reductions on many ship and bus routes.

## BANKS & MONEY

Banks are open from 9am to 3:30pm on weekdays, Thu until 5pm. The fees for exchanging currency vary by bank, but they are generally quite high. The Forex branches in Oslo and Bergen charge 50 NOK for each exchange transaction. There are many cash dispensers. Master Card and Visa are accepted in most hotels, restaurants, garages and major shops. There are no limits to the amount of foreign cash that can be brought into the country.

# From arrival to weather

**Your holiday from start to finish: the most important addresses and information for your Norway trip**

## CUSTOMS

Your luggage will be checked through to your final destination but the traveller must collect it at the first Norwegian airport, take it through customs and hand it in again at a domestic flight counter. Hunting weapons must be declared.

People of 18 years of age can import alcohol but you have to be at least 20 to bring in spirits; the limits are 1 L of spirits, 1.5 L of wine and 2 L of beer. It is forbidden to export plants and rare animals (including the eggs of threatened bird species). Exports of fish and fish products are limited to 15 kg per person.

It is worth buying things at the duty-free shop: more than half of the 25 percent VAT will be refunded at the border. There are around 4,000 tax-free shops in Norway. The minimum purchase is 315 NOK and the goods must be in their original packing. Remember to ask for a *Global Refund Cheque* when making your purchases.

The following articles can be imported tax-free into the EU: 200 cigarettes or 50 cigars or 250 grams of tobacco, 1 L of spirits with more than 22 percent alcoholic content or 2 litres with less, as well as goods valued at up to £ 390.

## DOMESTIC FLIGHTS

The Dash 8s of the Widerøe Airline land in the most remote corners of the country. SAS flies to the major airports. If you plan to travel in summer, it is a good idea to check the internet. *www.flysas.no | www. norwegian.no | www.wideroe.no*.

## DRIVING

The maximum speed in built-up areas is 50 km/h (in residential areas, often 30), on motorways 90, on main roads 80, with a caravan 70 km/h (without brakes 60). Dipped headlights are obligatory at all times. The blood alcohol limit is 0.2. It is compulsory for everybody to wear seat belts and children under the age of four require special seats. Passing points on single-lane roads are indicated with an "M". In winter, good winter tyres and snow chains are essential. *Information on closed roads: tel. 175* (the computer only speaks Norwegian at the beginning but don't hang up!). *NAF Automobile Club breakdown assistance: tel. 0 85 05*

**TOLL ROADS**: The *bompenger* ranges from 10 to 160 NOK (for bridges and tunnels). Information about the ways to pay the tolls is provided at most stations in three languages. The best thing to do is to open an AutoPASS account with a credit card on-line before departing for Norway at *www.autopass.no*. The visitor's pass agreement is valid for a maximum of two months with a prepayment of 300 NOK or 1,000 NOK depending on car size that will be deducted from your credit card after you pass through the first toll station. If you use up your initial prepayment, another prepayment amount will be booked to your credit card the next time you pass through a payment point. You can get a refund of any unused amount 85 days after your prepayment.

## ELECTRICITY

220 volt alternating current with the (type C & F) Europlug.

## EMBASSIES & CONSULATES

**BRITISH EMBASSY**
*Thomas Heftyes Gate 8 | 0244 Oslo | tel.: (47) 23 13 27 00 | www.gov.uk/world/organisations/british-embassy-oslo*

**EMBASSY OF THE UNITED STATES**
*Morgedalsvegen 36 | 0378 Oslo | switchboard: (47) 23 96 05 55 | no.usembassy.gov*

# BUDGETING

| Hot dog | from £ 2.40/$ 3.20 at most petrol stations and snack bars |
|---|---|
| Coffee | from £ 2.40/$ 3.20 for a cup |
| Beer | from £ 7.90/$ 10.70 for ½ L in a restaurant |
| Salmon | £ 18.50/$ 25 for 1kg of smoked salmon |
| Petrol | approx. £ 1.57/$ 2.13 for 1 litre of regular petrol |
| Pullover | from £ 160/$ 220 for a genuine Norwegian pullover |

**EMBASSY OF CANADA**
*Wergelandsveien 7 (4th floor) | 0244 Oslo | (47) 22 99 53 00 | www.canadainternational.gc.ca/norway-norvege/*

## EMERGENCY SERVICES

*Police: tel. 112*
*Fire brigade: tel. 110*
*Medical emergencies: tel. 113*

## EVERYMAN'S RIGHT

The *allemannsrett* permits everybody to move freely in the non-cultivated countryside – even on private property – and spend up to two nights there. People, animals and nature must not be disturbed in any way and you must keep a distance of at least 150 m/492 ft to the next inhabited house. Certain sections of the law have been rescinded in some national parks.

## HEALTH

Almost all medication requires a prescription. A foreign prescription won't do you any good in Norway so take any important medication you need with you. Headache tablets and nose drops, however, can be bought at the checkout in food shops. All major towns have a community *legevakt* (medical station). If you have a European Health Insurance Card (EHIC) you will have to pay the same excess as Norwegians (141 NOK; 238 NOK in the evening or at night). Dentists must be paid in full (350–1500 NOK). There are ticks in Norway. In contrast, the fox tapeworm is not widely spread which means you can eat the blueberries and cloudberries on picking them. In the interior and in Finnmark, mosquito nets and a good mosquito cream are essential.

## HOTELS & CABINS

Hotel rooms are usually cheaper in summer and hotel passes such as the *Fjord Pass* give you additional discounts. But, even if you don't have a pass, ask for lower rates. In the larger cities a double room costs 900–1500 NOK per night, without discount, and an average of 850 NOK in smaller hotels and pensions. All hotels provide breakfast buffets.

*Gjestgiveri*, *pensjon* and *fjellstue* offer budget overnight stays outside cities. The latter are the hikers' favourites – along with the cabins run by the *DNT (Den Norske Turistforeningen | www.turistfore-ningen.no | discounts with DNT card for 660 NOK)* – and hotel comforts are starting to make themselves felt even here. There are all standards of cabins: the most basic for 4–6 people costs from 4,000 NOK per week in the off-season (up to 10,000 NOK in the high season). The simplest camping cabin costs 350 NOK per night, larger ones with bath and kitchen as much as 1,400 NOK.

*Rorbus* are traditional Norwegian coastal dwellings that stand right on the water. There are a great many on the Lofoten – and, if you make it that far, you should spend some time in one of the most popular fishing villages in the group of islands: in *Henningsvær (tel. 76 06 60 00 | www.henningsvaer-rorbuer.no)*. If you would like to stay directly on the sea, but you don't want to drive that far, a beautiful *rorbu* complex can also be found on the island of *Sotra* off the coast of Bergen *(Glesvær Rorbu | tel. 97 11 03 36 | www.glesver-rorbu.no)*.

## INFORMATION

### INNOVATION NORWAY

*West End House, 11 Hills place | W1F 7SE London | Tel. +44 (0) 20 7389 8800 | www.visitnorway.com*

*www.norway.no* is Norway's official internet portal providing information on travelling, culture, politics and social matters, as well as studying and working in Norway.

There are good sites on western Norway and the fjords *(www.fjordnorway.com)* and the three most northern administrative regions *(www.nordnorge.com)*. *www.olavsrosa.no* gives information on the major sights and *www.yr.no* the current weather.

## MEDIA

Many cabins have television and satellite antennas. In the *Narvesen* kiosks in Oslo, Bergen and other major cities, you will find a selection of English-language newspapers and magazines.

## OPENING HOURS

Most shops are open Mon–Fri from 9am or 10am until 5pm and close earlier on Saturday. In the cities, most supermarkets are now open Mon–Fri 9am–11pm and Sat until 6pm. When you are out in the countryside, you should make sure to stock up on the basics during the regular opening hours, Mon–Fri 9am–5pm, Sat until 3pm. At other times, the centrally-located petrol stations stock a good selection of basic grocery items in addition to hot dogs and hamburgers.

## PHONES & MOBILE PHONES

All telephone numbers have eight digits and there are no dialling codes. The code for calling Norway from abroad is 0047. To call other countries from Norway, dial the country code (UK 0044, US 001, Ireland 00353), the dialling code without 0 and then the telephone number. With your mobile phone, dial + instead of the 00 before the country code.

In Norway, there are more mobile phone subscriptions than Norwegians but renting a phone is complicated and cannot be recommended. Since roaming surcharges ended in 2017 for all mobile network operators, you only need to pay domestic rates in Norway. As a member of the European Economic Area, Norway also agreed to this EU regulation. This also applies to SMS, MMS and mobile data volumes.

The most important telephone companies in Norway are Telenor (www.

## CURRENCY CONVERTER

| £ | NOK | NOK | £ |
|---|-----|-----|---|
| 10 | 108 | 100 | 9 |
| 20 | 219 | 200 | 18 |
| 30 | 329 | 300 | 27 |
| 40 | 439 | 400 | 36 |
| 50 | 549 | 500 | 45 |
| 60 | 658 | 600 | 55 |
| 70 | 768 | 700 | 64 |
| 80 | 878 | 800 | 73 |
| 90 | 987 | 900 | 82 |

| $ | NOK | NOK | $ |
|---|-----|-----|---|
| 10 | 81 | 100 | 12 |
| 20 | 162 | 200 | 25 |
| 30 | 243 | 300 | 37 |
| 40 | 324 | 400 | 49 |
| 50 | 406 | 500 | 62 |
| 60 | 486 | 600 | 74 |
| 70 | 568 | 700 | 86 |
| 80 | 649 | 800 | 99 |
| 90 | 730 | 900 | 111 |

For current exchange rates see www.xe.com

telenor.no, only in Norwegian ), Tele 2 (www.tele2.com, in English) and NetCom (www.netcom.no, only in Norwegian).

## PRICES & CURRENCY

100 Norwegian Kroner (NOK) are the equivalent of around £ 9 or US$12. It is subdivided into 100 øre. Purchasing power is not one of Norway's strong points and this is particularly apparent when buying food. Having fun is an expensive business, too: half a litre of beer in a pub costs at least 85 NOK, a good meal 330 NOK with an additional 380 NOK for a bottle of wine.

## PUBLIC TRANSPORT

### BUSES

Norway has many cross-country, regional and local buses that reach every corner of the country (connections: www.nor-way.no).

### FERRIES

Schedules for the regional ferry companies: www.norled.no, for western Norway www.fjord1.no; for central Norway www.kystriksveien.no/?page=ferjeruter; for northern Norway www.boreal.no.

### TRAINS

The network of the Norwegian National Railway (NSB) with almost 4,300 km/3,400 miles is not very tightly knit but, especially when travelling long distances, a train journey can be a lot of fun (generous open-plan carriages, comfortable seats and beds). It is a good idea to plan well ahead: tickets are available for 249 NOK if purchased 90 days in advance; if you wait longer, the price rises to 299 and later to 449 NOK.

## TIPPING

You should only tip if the service warrants it (maximum: 10 percent).

## WEATHER, WHEN TO GO

The climate is the same as the Norwegian countryside: it changes all the time and is rather unpredictable. In a country that stretches for 1,800 km/1,125 miles and has a mighty mountain range as a weather divide, it comes as no surprise that the east, west, north and south very rarely have the same weather. It is not unusual to have an Atlantic low in the south but a Siberian high in the north. The climatic instability will also affect your luggage: be prepared for rain and soggy ground when you are hiking in the middle of summer. And, even if the weather is calm, make sure that lifejackets, maps and GPS are always at hand when you are on a boat tour.

## YOUTH HOSTELS

There are around 70 youth hostels *(vandrerhjem)* in Norway. Beds cost 250 NOK for members; non-members pay an additional 25 NOK. Breakfast or a lunch packet is available for 50 NOK. More information is available at *hihostels.no* or from *Norske Vandrerhjem (Haraldsheimveien 4 | Box 53 | Grefsen | 0409 Oslo | tel. 23 12 45 10)*.

## WEATHER IN OSLO

| | Jan | Feb | March | April | May | June | July | Aug | Sept | Oct | Nov | Dec |
|---|---|---|---|---|---|---|---|---|---|---|---|---|
| **Daytime temperatures in °C/°F** | −2/28 | −1/30 | 4/39 | 10/50 | 16/61 | 20/68 | 22/72 | 21/70 | 16/61 | 9/48 | 3/37 | 0/32 |
| **Nighttime temperatures in °C/°F** | −7/19 | −7/19 | −4/25 | 1/34 | 6/43 | 10/50 | 13/55 | 12/54 | 8/46 | 3/37 | −1/30 | −4/25 |
| ☀ | 2 | 3 | 4 | 6 | 7 | 8 | 7 | 7 | 5 | 3 | 1 | 1 |
| ☂ | 8 | 7 | 5 | 7 | 7 | 10 | 11 | 11 | 10 | 10 | 12 | 10 |
| ≈ | 3/37 | 2/35 | 3/37 | 5/41 | 9/48 | 13/55 | 16/61 | 17/63 | 15/59 | 11/52 | 7/45 | 5/41 |

☀ Sunshine hours/day　🌂 Precipitation days/month　≋ Water temperature in °C/°F　**129**

# USEFUL PHRASES NORWEGIAN

## PRONUNCIATION

In this guide to phrases in the main Norwegian language, *bokmål*, simplified assistance in pronouncing the words has been added in square brackets. Note also that the vowel marked "ü" in the pronunciation guide is spoken as "ee" with rounded lips, like the "u" in French "tu", -e at the end of a word is a syllable spoken like the "e" in "the", and "g" is pronounced as in "get".

### IN BRIEF

| | |
|---|---|
| Yes/No/Maybe | Ja/Nei/Kanskje [ya/nayi/kansh-e] |
| Please | Vær så snill [vair sho snill] |
| Thank you | Takk [tak] |
| Excuse me, please/ Pardon? | Unnskyld [ünnshüll]/Hva sa du? [va sa dü] |
| May I...?/ | Kan jeg...? [kann yayi] |
| I would like to.../ | Jeg vil gjerne... [yayi vill yern-e]/ |
| Have you got...? | Har du (noen)... ? [har dü (nuen)] |
| How much is... | Hva koster... ? [va koster] |
| I (don't) like that | Det liker jeg (ikke) [de leeker yayi [ick-e]] |
| good/bad/broken/ | bra [bra]/dårlig [dorli]/ødelagt [erdelagt]/ |
| doesn't work | fungerer ikke [fungerer ick-e] |
| too much/much/little | for mye [for mü-e]/mye [mü-e]/lite [leet-e] |
| all/nothing | alt [alt]/ingenting [ingenting] |
| Help!/Attention!/ | Hjelp! [yelp]/Pass på! [pass po]/ |
| Caution! | Forsiktig! [forzikti] |
| ambulance/police/fire brigade | sykebil [zük-e-beel]/politi [politi]/ brannvesen [brannvayzen] |
| prohibition/forbidden | Forbud/forbudt [forbütt] |
| danger/dangerous | Fare [far-e]/farlig [farli] |

### GREETINGS, FAREWELL

| | |
|---|---|
| Good morning!/afternoon/ Hello! | God morgen! [gu morn]/God dag! [gu dag]/ Hei! [high] |
| Good evening!/night! | God kveld! [gu kvell]/God natt! [gu natt] |
| goodbye!/See you | Ha det! [ha de] |
| My name is... | Jeg heter... [yayi hayter] |
| What's your name? | Hva heter du? [va hayter dü] |
| I'm from... | Jeg er fra... [yayi er fra] |

# Snakker du norsk?

**"Do you speak Norwegian?"** This guide will help you to say the basic words and phrases in Norwegian.

## DATE AND TIME

| | |
|---|---|
| Monday/Tuesday | mandag [mandag]/tirsdag [teersdag] |
| Wednesday/Thursday | onsdag [unsdag]/torsdag [toorsdag] |
| Friday/Saturday | fredag[fraydag]/lørdag [lerdag] |
| Sunday/working day | søndag [zerndag]/ukedag[ük-edag] |
| holiday | helligdag [hellidag] |
| today/tomorrow/yesterday | i dag [ee dag]/i morgen [ee morn]/i går [ee gor] |
| hour/minute | time [teem-e]/minutt [minütt] |
| day/night/week | dag [dag]/natt[natt]/uke [ük-e] |
| month/year | måned [mon-ed]/år [oar] |
| What time is it? | Hva er klokken? [va air klocken?] |
| It's three o'clock/ | Klokken er tre [klocken air tre]/ |
| It's half past three | Klokken er halv fire [klocken air hal feer-e] |

## TRAVEL

| | |
|---|---|
| open/closed | åpent [opent]/stengt [stengt] |
| entrance/vehicle entrance | inngang [ingang]/innkjørsel [inkyersel] |
| exit/vehicle exit | utgang [ütgang]/utkjørsel [ütkyersel] |
| departure/arrival | avgang [avgang]/ankomst [ankommst] |
| toilets | toaletter [twaletter] |
| Where is...?/Where are...? | Hvor er...? [voor air] |
| left/right | venstre [venstr-e]/høyre [her-ir-e] |
| straight ahead/back | rett fram [rett fram]/tilbake [tillbaak-e] |
| close/far | nært [nairt]/langt (unna) [langt (ünna) |
| bus/tram | buss [büss]/trikk [trick] |
| underground/taxi/cab | T-bane [te-baan-e]/drosje [drosh-e] |
| stop/cab stand | stoppested [stopp-e-sted]/ drosjeholdeplass [drosh-e-holleplass] |
| parking lot/ parking garage | parkeringsplass [parkeringsplass]/ parkeringshus[parkeringshüss] |
| street map/map | bykart [bükart]/kart [kart] |
| train station/ harbour/airport | jernbanestasjon [yernbaan-e-stashon]/ havn [haavn]/flyplass [flüplass] |
| ticket/supplement | billett [beelett]/påslag [poshlag] |
| single/return | enkel [enkel]/tur-retur [tür-retür] |
| train/track/platform | tog [tog]/spor [spoor]/rute [rüt-e] |
| I would like to rent... | Jeg vil gjerne leie... [yayi vill yern-e ly-e] |
| a car/a bicycle/a boat | en bil [en beel]/sykkel [zükkel]/båt [boat] |
| petrol/gas station | bensinstasjon [benzinstashon] |
| breakdown/repair shop | skade/verksted [shaad-e/vairksted] |

## FOOD & DRINK

| | |
|---|---|
| Could you please book a table for tonight for four? | Vi vil gjerne bestille et bord for fire personer til i kveld. [vee vill yairn-e bestill-e et boor for feer-e perzooner till ee kvell] |
| The menu, please | Kan jeg få menyen? [kann yayi fo menü-en] |
| Could I please have...? | Kunne jeg få...? [künn-e yayi fo] |
| salt/pepper/sugar | salt [zalt]/pepper [pepper]/sukker [zucker] |
| vinegar/oil | eddik [eddick]/olje [uly-e] |
| milk/cream/lemon | melk [melk]/fløte [flert-e]/sitron [zitroon] |
| with/without ice | med [may]/uten is [üten eess] |
| vegetarian/allergy | vegetarianer [vegetarianer]/allergi [allergee] |
| May I have the bill, please? | Jeg vil gjerne betale [yayi vill yairn-e betal-e] |

## SHOPPING

| | |
|---|---|
| I'd like.../ | Jeg vil gjerne... [yayi vill yairn-e]/ |
| I'm looking for... | Jeg leter etter... [yayi layter etter] |
| pharmacy/chemist | apotek/parfymeri [apotayk/parfümeree] |
| baker/market | bakeri [backeree]/torget [torg] |
| shopping centre/ | handlesenter [hand-le-zenter]/ |
| department store | varehus [var-e-hüs] |
| supermarket | supermarked [süpermark-ed] |
| more/less | mer [mair]/mindre [mindr-e] |
| organically grown | biologisk dyrket [bioologish dürket] |

## ACCOMMODATION

| | |
|---|---|
| I have booked a room | Jeg har bestilt et rom [yai har bestilt ett room] |
| single room | enkeltrom [enkeltroom] |
| double room | dobbeltrom [dobbeltroom] |
| breakfast/half board/ | frokost [frookost]/halvpensjon [halpanshon]/ |
| full board (American plan) | fullpension [füllpanshon] |
| the front/ | mot framsiden [moot frammzeeden]/ |
| seafront/ | mot sjøen [moot shern]/ |
| lakefront | mot innsjøen [moot innshern] |
| key/room card | nøkkel/nøkkelkort [nerckel/nerckelkoort] |
| luggage/suitcase/ | bagasje [bagash-e]/koffert [kooffert]/ |
| bag | veske [vesk-e]/bag [beg] |

## BANKS, MONEY & CREDIT CARDS

| | |
|---|---|
| bank/ATM | bank [bank]/minibank [minibank] |
| pin code | bankkode [bankkood-e] |
| I'd like to change... | Jeg vil gjerne veksle... [yayi vill yairn-e vek-sle...] |

| cash/credit card | kontant [kontant]/kredittkort [kreditkoort] |
| bill/coin | seddel [zeddel]/mynt [münt] |

## HEALTH

| doctor/dentist/ paediatrician | lege [legg-e]/tannlege [tannlegg-e]/ barnelege [baan-e-legg-e] |
| hospital/emergency clinic | sykehus [sük-e-hüs/legevakt [legg-e-vakt] |
| fever/pain | feber [fayber]/smerter [smairter] |
| diarrhoea/nausea | diaré [deearay]/kvalme [kvalm-e] |
| pain reliever/ tablet | smertestillende [smairt-e-stillend-e]/ tablett [tablett] |

## POST, TELECOMMUNICATIONS & MEDIA

| stamp/postcard | frimerke [freemairk-e]/postkort [postkort] |
| I need a landline phone card/ prepaid card for my -mobile | Jeg trenger et telefonkort/kontantkort [yayi trenger ett telefonkort/kontantkort] |
| Where can I find internet access? | Hvor er nærmeste internettilgang? [voor er nairmest-e internettilgang] |
| Do I need a special area code? | Må jeg slå et spesielt nummer først? [mo yayi shlo ett speseelt nummer ferst] |
| dial/ connection/engaged | slå et nummer [shlo ett nummer]/ linje [liny-e]/opptatt [upptatt] |
| internet connection/wifi | internettilkobling [internett-tilkoblin] |

## LEISURE, SPORTS & BEACH

| (rescue) hut/avalanche | hytte [hütt-e]/ras [raz] |
| cable car/chair lift | taubane [towbaan-e]/stolheis [stoolhice] |
| low tide/high tide/ current | fjære [fyair-e]/flo [floo]/ strøm [strerm] |
| beach/bathing beach | strand [stran]/sjøbad [sherbad] |

## NUMBERS

| 0 | null [nüll] | 10 | ti [tee] |
|---|---|---|---|
| 1 | en [ayn] | 11 | elleve [ellv-e] |
| 2 | to [too] | 12 | tolv [toll] |
| 3 | tre [tre] | 20 | tjue/tyve [chü-e/tü-ve] |
| 4 | fire [feer-e] | 100 | hundre [hün-dre] |
| 5 | fem [fem] | 200 | tohundre [toohün-dre] |
| 6 | seks [zeks] | 1000 | ettusen [ettüsen] |
| 7 | sju/syv [shü/züv] | 2000 | totusen [tootüsen] |
| 8 | åtte [ott-e] | ½ | en halv [ayn hal] |
| 9 | ni [nee] | ¼ | en kvart [ayn kvart] |

# ROAD ATLAS

The green line indicates the Discovery Tour "Norway at a glance"
The blue line indicates the other Discovery Tours

All tours are also marked on the pull-out map

# Exploring Norway

The map on the back cover shows how the area has been sub-divided

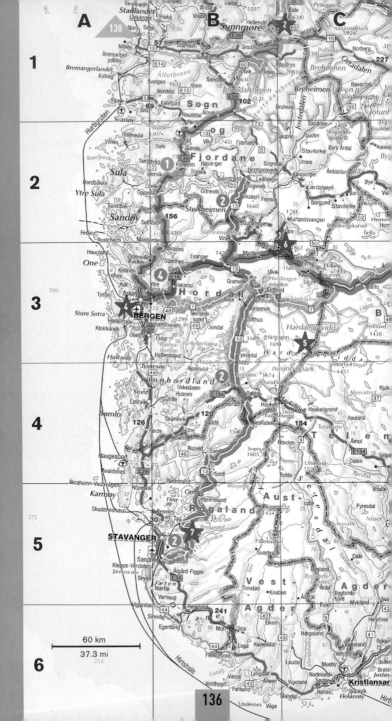

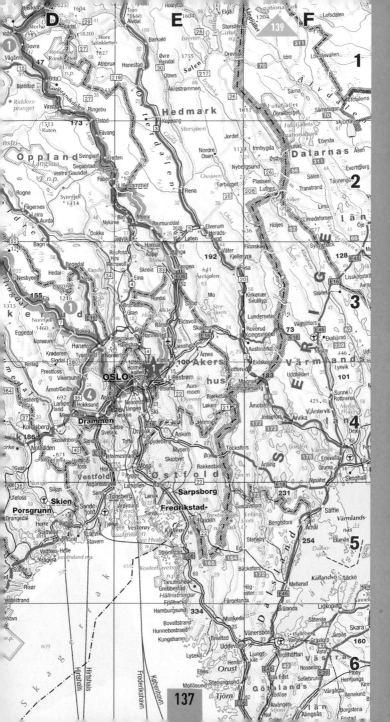

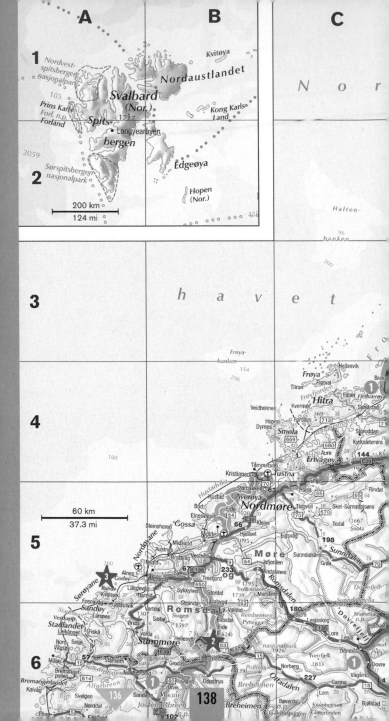

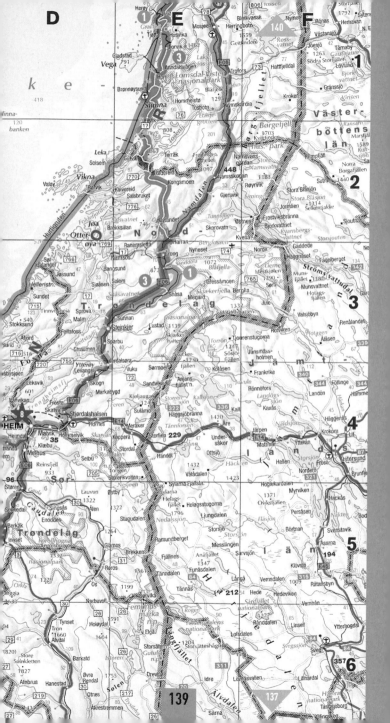

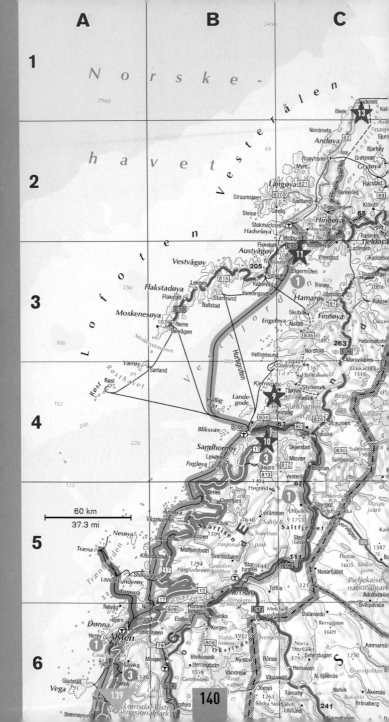

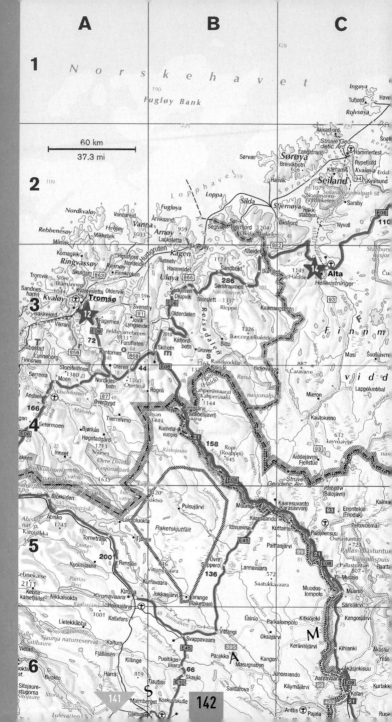

N o r s k e h a v e t

Fugløy Bank

Ingøya
Tufjord
Rolvsøya

Akkarfjord
Struve Geo detic Arc
Langstrand  Hammerfest
Sørvær  Breivikbotn  Sørøya  Karnámn  Rypefjord
Hasvik  656  Kvalåva Erdal
Kvalsund

Loppa  Silda  Seiland
Sør-  Stjernøya  1079  Seilanda nasjonalpark
Segsvik  Bjerfjord  Øksfjord  Nordmanns-  fjordnokken
Nyvoll  Saraby

Nordkvaløy  Vannareid  Fugløya  Olsfjordhåken  40  E06  882  110

Rebbenesøy  Helgøy  Vanna  1033  Árviksand  959  Sør-  61  Stabbur
Mikkelvik  Arnøy  Skjervøy  Alteidet  nasjo

Komagvik  Hessfjord  Hamneidet  117  Sandbukt  1149  14  Alta
Ringvassøy  Reinøy  Kågen  Russell  286  Burfjord  Halddi  Helleristninger
Tromvik  Store  B863  Finnkroken  Uløya  866  93  Finn m
Skulgam  Blåmannen  Sørkjosen  Sørstraumen  103  F
Sandnes-  1044  Tromsø  Djupvik  Storslett  1337  Naviftjonen  Kvænangsbtn
hamn  Kvaløysletta Olderdal  12  Svensby  91  Ricppe
Kvaløy  Fagernes  Jovik Lyngseide  Olderdalen  T326  Masi  Šuošjávri
Gibostad  E08  1596  Báccegælhaldde  887  Čáravárre
Bakkejord  72  Jiekkevarrebreen  2018  v i d d
Vikran  1833  64  Kåfjord-  Bitto  Imo  887
Lurineboard  B858  Furuflaten  botn  Gruvep
Finnsnes  868  Skibotn  S  Rašdiddar-  Bidjovagge
Serreisa  Oteren  44  Haldde  Reisa  nasjonalp  Mieron  Lappoluobbal
Storsteinnes  1380  E08  Kåfperusvaara  1144
Andselv  Moen  Nordkjos-  1360  Rognli  (Kahperusak)  Kautokeino
166  botn  Otertind  Čáravárre  632
E08  Øverbygd  87  Guolasjávri  Lávvoáive
gan  Målselva  Tverrelvmo  Kummavuopio  158  Ropi  93
Setermoen  Bjørkås  1444  (Roahppi)  Aiddejávrre
Høgstadgård  112  945  Fjellstue
1713  Kumma  Struve
Innset  Njunes  vuopio  Rástojaure  E08  Geodetic Arc  Paitojärvi
Øvre Dividal  (Balojävri)  Enontekiö
nasjonalpark  Leina  Palojoensuu  (Enodak)  Kalma
1633  vatne  Malatno  93
Bjørkliden  saksto  Pulsujärvi  Kaaresuvanto  Ounastunturi
Abisk  141  (Karasavvon)  723
Abisko  Torneträsk  Láimoluokta  Idivuoma  Kaaresuando  Pallas-  Yllästuntu
naf p.  1745  Raketskjutfält  Kurtalmen  Palojoensuu  kansallispuis
Kåtojåkka  Tjälme  Paittasjärvi  E08  Pallastunturi
Tornetrask  Idivuoma  99  807
Rautas  125  Øvre  Lannavaara  Yli-Muonio
Kuolasjaure  200  Rensjön  Soppero  107  572  Muodos-  Muonio
Paittas-  836  Vittangivaara  136  Saatukkavaara  lompolo  Särkijärvi
kebnekaise  järvi  Kitkiöjoki  Kangosjärvi
2111  Kiruna  Jukkasjärvi  M
kaisefjällr  Kurravaara  Esrange  Kangosjärvi   Kihlanki
Nikkaluokta  Kiirunavaara  (Raketbas)  Keräntöjärvi  E08
1001  Holmajärvi  Áinio  Parkalompolo  Akäslor
Lietekkåbba  48  Tornealven  Oksajärvi  Akäsjokisuu  Ylläs
Kafixfors  Kitkiöjärvi  99
fallet  819  Vittangi  Kangos  Aareavaara  21
Satihaure  Kaitum  Svappavaara  Junosuando  Käymäjärvi  E08
Sjaunja naturreservat  Killinge  E45  395  Kolari
Vietas  Fjällåsen  Puoltikas-  Parakka  A  Masugnsbyn
vaara  66  Saittarova  Anttis  Pajala  21
Buckto  Harrå  Tjautjas  E10  Skaulo
Sitojaure-  Stora  Koskullskulle
stugorna  S  Malmberget  142
Sitojaure  Gällivare  Lulevatten  Rugt

141

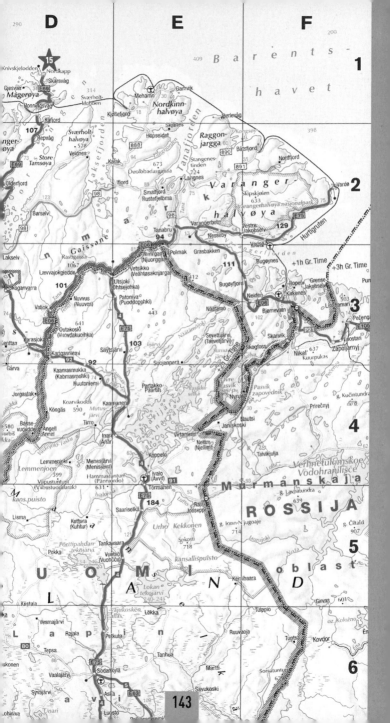

# KEY TO ROAD ATLAS

|  |  |  |
|---|---|---|
| Autobahn, mehrspurige Straße - in Bau<br>Highway, multilane divided road - under construction | | Autoroute, route à plusieurs voies - en construction<br>Autosnelweg, weg met meer rijstroken - in aanleg |
| Fernverkehrsstraße - in Bau<br>Trunk road - under construction | | Route à grande circulation - en construction<br>Weg voor interlokaal verkeer - in aanleg |
| Hauptstraße<br>Principal highway | | Route principale<br>Hoofdweg |
| Nebenstraße<br>Secondary road | | Route secondaire<br>Overige verharde wegen |
| Fahrweg, Piste<br>Practicable road, track | | Chemin carrossable, piste<br>Weg, piste |
| Straßennummerierung<br>Road numbering | E20 11 70 26 | Numérotage des routes<br>Wegnummering |
| Entfernungen in Kilometer<br>Distances in kilometers | 259<br>130    129 | Distances en kilomètres<br>Afstand in kilometers |
| Höhe in Meter - Pass<br>Height in meters - Pass | 1365 | Altitude en mètres - Col<br>Hoogte in meters - Pas |
| Eisenbahn - Eisenbahnfähre<br>Railway - Railway ferry | | Chemin de fer - Ferry-boat<br>Spoorweg - Spoorpont |
| Autofähre - Schifffahrtslinie<br>Car ferry - Shipping route | | Bac autos - Ligne maritime<br>Autoveer - Scheepvaartlijn |
| Wichtiger internationaler Flughafen - Flughafen<br>Major international airport - Airport | ✈ ✈ | Aéroport importante international - Aéroport<br>Belangrijke internationale luchthaven - Luchthaven |
| Internationale Grenze - Provinzgrenze<br>International boundary - Province boundary | | Frontière internationale - Limite de Province<br>Internationale grens - Provinciale grens |
| Unbestimmte Grenze<br>Undefined boundary | | Frontière d'Etat non définie<br>Rijksgrens onbepaalt |
| Zeitzonengrenze<br>Time zone boundary | -4h Greenwich Time<br>-3h Greenwich Time | Limite de fuseau horaire<br>Tijdzone-grens |
| Hauptstadt eines souveränen Staates<br>National capital | **OSLO** | Capitale nationale<br>Hoofdstad van een souvereine staat |
| Hauptstadt eines Bundesstaates<br>Federal capital | **Nancy** | Capitale d'un état fédéral<br>Hoofdstad van een deelstat |
| Sperrgebiet<br>Restricted area | | Zone interdite<br>Verboden gebied |
| Nationalpark<br>National park | | Parc national<br>Nationaal park |
| Antikes Baudenkmal<br>Ancient monument | ∴ | Monument antiques<br>Antiek monument |
| Sehenswertes Kulturdenkmal<br>Interesting cultural monument | * Chambord | Monument culturel interéssant<br>Bezienswaardig cultuurmonument |
| Sehenswertes Naturdenkmal<br>Interesting natural monument | * Gorges<br>du Tarn | Monument naturel interéssant<br>Bezienswaardig natuurmonument |
| Brunnen<br>Well | ‿ | Puits<br>Bron |
| MARCO POLO Erlebnistour 1<br>MARCO POLO Discovery Tour 1 | | MARCO POLO Tour d'aventure 1<br>MARCO POLO Avontuurlijke Routes 1 |
| MARCO POLO Erlebnistouren<br>MARCO POLO Discovery Tours | | MARCO POLO Tours d'aventure<br>MARCO POLO Avontuurlijke Routes |
| MARCO POLO Highlight | ★1 | MARCO POLO Highlight |

# FOR YOUR NEXT TRIP...

# MARCO POLO TRAVEL GUIDES

Travel with
**Insider
Tips**

# INDEX

This index lists all places, destinations and sights featured in this guide. Numbers in bold indicate a main entry.

# WRITE TO US

e-mail: info@marcopologuides.co.uk

Did you have a great holiday?
Is there something on your mind?
Whatever it is, let us know!
Whether you want to praise, alert us
to errors or give us a personal tip –
MARCO POLO would be pleased to
hear from you.
We do everything we can to provide the
very latest information for your trip.

Nevertheless, despite all of our authors'
thorough research, errors can creep in.
MARCO POLO does not accept any
liability for this. Please contact us by
e-mail or post.

MARCO POLO Travel Publishing Ltd
Pinewood, Chineham Business Park
Crockford Lane, Chineham
Basingstoke, Hampshire RG24 8AL
United Kingdom

## PICTURE CREDITS

Cover photograph: Reine, Lofoten (Schapowalow: H.-P. Huber)
Photographs: DuMont Bildarchiv: U. Bernhart (100/101), Modrow (68, 76); Getty Images: P. Adams (64/65), alxpin (72, 123), J. Kadaj (43), H. Luijting (34), T. Moore (3), D. Ryle (120/121), K. Westgård (70/71), J. Wlodarczyk (4 top, 48/49), S. Wongsanuphat (54); Getty Images/ Cultura: Apeloga AB (19 bottom); Getty Images/ Digital Vision (121); Getty Images/ EyeEM: K. Kohanova (19 top); huber-images: M. Borchi (8), S. Damm (12/13), S. Forster (91), Gräfenhain (80/81, 134/135), M. Rellini (97), L. Vaccarella (9); Laif: T. Babovic (53, 88, 122 bottom), N. Bibel (6), H. Bode (26/27, 50), M. Galli (14, 92/93, 98), G. Hänel (75, 119), I. C. Hendel (120), M. Kirchgessner (29), S. Multhaupt (30, 38, 44, 122 top); Laif/ Aurora (23); Laif/ hemis.fr: E. Berthier (25), P. Hauser (31); Look: H. Dressler (94); Look/ age fotostock (63); mauritius images: U. Bernhart (11, 66), Novarc/ J. Heuckeroth (111), B. Römmelt (82), S. Schurr (20/21), J. Warburton-Lee (4 bottom, 86/87), A. Werth (57); mauritius images/ age fotostock (10, 85, 112/113), R. T. Sigurdsson (18 bottom); mauritius images/ Alamy: (2, 18 top, 18 centre, 47, 58, 79, 106, 108), Dorling Kindersley (28 left), INSADCO Photography (30/31), P. K. Lloyd (7), R. Richardson (37), Utterström Photography (40); mauritius images/ Cultura: P. L. Harvey (17); mauritius images/ imagebroker: Handl (28 right), T. Krämer (115), A. Schnurer (60); mauritius images/ robertharding (5); mauritius images/ Science Faction (flap right); mauritius images/ VIEW Pictures (flap left); Schapowalow: H.-P. Huber (1); vario images/ Cultura (116/117); vario images/ sodapix (32/33)

## 3rd Edition – fully revised and updated 2019

Worldwide Distribution: Marco Polo Travel Publishing Ltd, Pinewood, Chineham Business Park,
Crockford Lane, Basingstoke, Hampshire RG24 8AL, United Kingdom. Email: sales@marcopolouk.com
© MAIRDUMONT GmbH & Co. KG, Ostfildern
Chief editor: Marion Zorn
Author: Jens-Uwe Kumpch; co-author: Julia Fellinger; editor: Corinna Walkenhorst
Programme supervision: Lucas Forst-Gill, Susanne Heimburger, Tamara Hub, Johanna Jiranek, Nikolai Michaelis, Kristin Wittemann, Tim Wohlbold; Picture editor: Gabriele Forst, Anja Schlatterer
What's hot: Julia Fellinger; Jens-Uwe Kumpch; wunder media, Munich
Cartography road atlas: © MAIRDUMONT, Ostfildern; Cartography pull-out map: © MAIRDUMONT, Ostfildern
Design front cover, p. 1, pull-out map cover: Karl Anders – Büro für Visual Stories, Hamburg; interior: milchhof:atelier, Berlin; Discovery Tours, p. 2/3: Susan Chaaban Dipl.-Des. (FH)
Translated from German by Susan Jones, Jennifer Walcoff Neuheiser; Prepress: writehouse, Cologne; InterMedia, Ratingen
Phrase book in cooperation with Ernst Klett Sprachen GmbH, Stuttgart, Editorial by
Pons Wörterbücher

All rights reserved. No part of this book may be reproduced, stored in a retrieval
system or transmitted in any form or by any means (electronic, mechanical, photo-
copying, recording or otherwise) without prior written permission from the
publisher. Printed in India

MIX
Paper from
responsible sources
FSC® C016779
FSC
www.fsc.org

# DOS & DON'TS ☝

**A few things you should bear in mind in Norway**

## DON'T UNDERESTIMATE NATURE

Hair-raising stories often make the headlines in summer of inappropriately dressed tourists getting lost in the mountains or of poorly planned fishing trips drifting into the open sea. Norway's nature should not be treated as a large fun park and visitors are encouraged to enjoy its beauty while also respecting its hidden risks. Make sure to plan your trips well and listen to the advice of locals.

## DO SAY "THANK YOU" FOR EVERYTHING

The little word *takk* is the basis for all politeness and is often a door opener. The Norwegians even thank you if you ask how they are. But, they never say "thanks for everything" – *takk for alt*. That is reserved for tombstones, wreath ribbons and obituaries. The Norwegians are much more precise about thanking: after a meal *takk for matten*, after a pleasant evening *takk for i kveld* and for the last get-together *takk for sist*.

## DON'T GET IMPATIENT

Norwegians do not push and shove and they certainly don't jump the queue. There is a widespread saying in the country *Ta det med ro* (all good things take time) and this applies everywhere. In busy places, a *kølapp* system (ticket system) is often in place to manage the waiting customers. When it's finally your turn, feel free to take all the time in the world.

## DON'T RISK A TRAFFIC FINE

Like to drive faster when you're on holiday? If you think Norwegian speed tickets won't reach you at home, you're wrong: foreign drivers are fined and the authorities in their home country informed. As little as 5 km/h too fast costs 750 NOK, if you're up to 15 km/h too fast in a 70 km/h zone, you'll have to pay 3,300 NOK. Talking on the phone without a hands-free set costs 1,650 NOK while parking in the wrong spot sets you back at least 500 NOK.

## DON'T PILE YOUR CAR UP WITH ALCOHOL

You're not prepared to pay the Norwegian price for alcohol and plan to bring your own beer, wine and spirits from home? Think again – unless you want to leave all your holiday cash at customs. The permissible import quota is four bottles of wine, six cans of beer and one bottle of spirits. Those who can do without spirits can take an extra two bottles of wine *(toll.no)*.

## DON'T STOCK UP FOR YOUR REFRIGERATOR AT HOME

Fishing is fun, but take the export restrictions on fish seriously (see "Travel Tips"). The fish stocks in the fjords are endangered; you can easily get into trouble with the customs authorities especially during high season when border controls are frequent and fines are heavy.